POPULATION HEALTH MANAGEMENT IN HEALTH CARE ORGANIZATIONS

ADVANCES IN HEALTH CARE MANAGEMENT

Series Editors: Leonard Friedman, Grant T. Savage, and Jim Goes

Recent Volumes:

ADVANCES IN HEALTH CARE MANAGEMENT
VOLUME 16

POPULATION HEALTH MANAGEMENT IN HEALTH CARE ORGANIZATIONS

EDITED BY

JENNIFER L. HEFNER
The Ohio State University, Columbus, OH, USA

TIMOTHY R. HUERTA
The Ohio State University, Columbus, OH, USA

ANN SCHECK McALEARNEY
The Ohio State University, Columbus, OH, USA

United Kingdom – North America – Japan
India – Malaysia – China

Emerald Group Publishing Limited
Howard House, Wagon Lane, Bingley BD16 1WA, UK

First edition 2014

British Library Cataloguing in Publication Data
A catalogue record for this book is available from the British Library

ISBN: 978-1-78441-197-8
ISSN: 1474-8231 (Series)

CONTENTS

SECTION II: PHM BETWEEN HEALTH CARE ORGANIZATIONS

SECTION III: PHM INTEGRATING HEALTH CARE ORGANIZATIONS AND OTHER FIELDS

SECTION IV: FACTORS IN PHM BEYOND THE MANAGEMENT OF HEALTH CARE ORGANIZATIONS

LIST OF CONTRIBUTORS

Alison Aldrich	Health Sciences Library, The Ohio State University, Columbus, OH, USA
Joan Bloom	School of Public Health, Health Policy and Management, University of California, Berkeley, Berkeley, CA, USA
Erik L. Carlton	Division of Health Systems Management and Policy, The University of Memphis School of Public Health, Memphis, TN, USA
Jami DelliFraine	Department of Health Administration, Virginia Commonwealth University, Richmond, VA, USA
Ebbin Dotson	Department of Community Health Sciences, University of Illinois at Chicago, Chicago, IL, USA
Connie Evashwick	CEA – Consulting and Evaluation Associates, San Diego, CA, USA
Edmund Funai	Wexner Medical Center, The Ohio State University Columbus, OH, USA
Laurel Geist	Division of Health Services Management and Policy, College of Public Health, The Ohio State University, Columbus, OH, USA
Richard P. Green	Design Management Program, Pratt Institute, New York, NY, USA
Kristine R. Hearld	Department of Health Services Administration, School of Health Professions, University of Alabama at Birmingham, Birmingham, AL, USA

Larry R. Hearld	Department of Health Services Administration, School of Health Professions, University of Alabama at Birmingham, Birmingham, AL, USA
Jennifer L. Hefner	Department of Family Medicine, College of Medicine, The Ohio State University, Columbus, OH, USA
Jeffrey Helton	Metropolitan State University of Denver, Denver, CO, USA
Tory H. Hogan	Department of Health Services Administration, School of Health Professions, University of Alabama at Birmingham, Birmingham, AL, USA
Timothy R. Huerta	Departments of Family Medicine and Biomedical Informatics, College of Medicine, The Ohio State University, Columbus, OH, USA
James Langabeer, II	The University of Texas, Houston, TX, USA
Tina Latimer	Wexner Medical Center, The Ohio State University, Columbus, OH, USA
Sarah Lewis	Health Services and Policy Analysis, University of California at Berkeley, Berkeley, CA, USA
Karen Love	Community Health Choice, Houston, TX, USA
Ann Scheck McAlearney	Department of Family Medicine, College of Medicine, The Ohio State University, Columbus, OH, USA
Susan Moffatt-Bruce	Wexner Medical Center, The Ohio State University, Columbus, OH, USA
Arash Naeim	School of Medicine, University of California, Los Angeles, CA, USA

Jennifer Rice	Health Services and Policy Analysis, University of California at Berkeley, Berkeley, CA, USA
Stephen Shortell	School of Public Health, Health Policy and Management, Haas School of Business, University of California, Berkeley, Berkeley, CA, USA
Cynthia J. Sieck	Department of Family Medicine, The Ohio State University, Columbus, OH, USA
Denise C. Tahara	Department of Health Policy and Management, School of Health Sciences and Practice, New York Medical College, Valhalla, NY, USA
Jason S. Turner	Department of Health Management and Policy, Saint Louis University, Saint Louis, MO, USA
Carolyn Watts	Department of Health Administration, Virginia Commonwealth University, Richmond, VA, USA
Randell K. Wexler	Family Medicine and Wexner Medical Center, The Ohio State University, Columbus, OH, USA
Thomas Wickizer	Division of Health Services Management and Policy, College of Public Health, The Ohio State University, Columbus, OH, USA

LIST OF REVIEWERS

Ann Chou
University of Oklahoma Health Sciences Center, Oklahoma, USA

Alison Cuellar
George Mason University, Virginia, USA

Jami DelliFraine
Virginia Commonwealth University, Virginia, USA

Fred van Eenennaam
Erasmus University Rotterdam, Rotterdam, The Netherlands; George Washington University, Washington, DC, USA

Eric Ford
Johns Hopkins University, Maryland, USA

Leonard Friedman
George Washington University, Washington, DC, USA

Mattia J. Gilmartin
New York University, New York, USA

Chris Harle
University of Florida, Florida, USA

Jeff Helton
Metro University of Denver, Colorado, USA

Deirdre McCaughey
The Pennsylvania State University, Pennsylvania, USA

Nir Menachemi
University of Alabama at Birmingham, Alabama, USA

Kathleen Montgomery
University of California, Riverside, California, USA

Ingrid Nembhard
Yale University, Connecticut, USA

Peter E. Rivard
Suffolk University, Massachusetts, USA

Grant Savage
University of Alabama at Birmingham, Alabama, USA

Valerie Yeager
Tulane University, Louisiana, USA

EDITORIAL ADVISORY BOARD

PREFACE

WHAT IS POPULATION HEALTH MANAGEMENT?

The mission of health care organizations has undergone a remarkable transformation from curing disease to caring for the well-being of populations. Population health differs from individual health because it connotes a higher level assessment of a group of people (Hacker & Walker, 2013). The group, or population, can be defined based on multiple criteria including geographic location, community membership, disease or treatment plan, or insurance claims linked to a provider (Magnan et al., 2012; McAlearney, 2002). In current health policy and management practice, the realms of population health and health services provision are converging, leading to the coining of the term "practice-based population health." This refers to the responsibility of primary care groups and networks for the health of their patient populations (Cusack, Knudson, Kronstadt, Singer, & Brown, 2010). While this responsibility has traditionally been confined to the illness-care needs of the population, in this conceptualization population health management (PHM) strategies are broader and include lifestyle management, demand management, disease management, catastrophic care management, and disability management (McAlearney, 2003).

The Health Maintenance Organizations of the 1990s are a classic example of the application of traditional population health management activities to health services provision. Current efforts to create Patient-Centered Medical Homes (PCMH) and Accountable Care Organizations (ACO) represent broader efforts to move organizational responsibilities toward population health and care management. While the traditional population management strategies are a critical element, current efforts take a broader definition of population health and incorporate new management strategies. Specifically, managers of primary care clinics, hospitals, and health systems must focus on building community partnerships with local non-profits, health departments, and both mental and social services agencies (Hacker & Walker, 2013; Magnan et al., 2012; McLellan et al., 2012). Managers must also fully utilize current health information technologies (HIT) and registries in order to identify and track attributed patient populations (Parton & Ravi, 2012). Other new population health management strategies include a focus on patient-centered care by incorporating the patient voice and preferences into the patient experience (Carman et al., 2013; Huerta et al., 2013), and altering the experience of patient care to address wellness and behavior changes as well as sick care (Hacker & Walker, 2013; Magnan et al., 2012).

The expansion of these population health management strategies stems from the fact that health care, the traditional purview of the health care system, accounts for only 20% of a population's health (Magnan et al., 2012). Health behaviors, increasingly a focus of the health care system, account for another 30%. Socioeconomic factors such as education, employment, social support, and community safety account for 40%, and the physical environment the remaining 10%. These factors are traditionally considered outside the purview of the health care system. However, successful population health management requires "not only medical services that are vertically integrated but also horizontally integrated health, education and social services that promote health in all policies, places, and daily activities" (Halfon & Conway, 2013). The health services sector can engage in this process through supportive community initiatives focusing on disease prevention, health and lifestyle education, healthy neighborhoods, and supportive communities (Hacker & Walker, 2013; Halfon & Conway, 2013).

From a management perspective, the new PHM is challenged by the increasing burden of chronic disease, the aging of the population, financial models that demand new types of services without payment models to support these services, and the increasing complexity of medical interventions. The PCMH and the ACO are two models of care transformation that position population health management as their central function. Implementation of a PCMH focuses on the transformation of the primary care system at the level of individual clinics, while organizing as an ACO engages entire health care systems to vertically integrate. Neither of these models of care transformation can be successful without shifting the provision of health care through the implementation of the new population health management strategies outlined earlier. Many of these transformations are underway in clinics and health systems across the country, and the successes and failures of these efforts are being carefully studied, including in the papers of this volume.

OVERVIEW OF THE PAPERS IN THIS VOLUME

Volume 16 of AHCM presents papers that explore population health management across various levels of the health care system employing multiple research designs: case studies, theoretical pieces, secondary data analysis, survey research, and qualitative methodologies. Aspects of health care organization discussed in the volume include the PCMH, ACOs, integration with the public health and mental health systems, hospital-physician alignment, and resource planning. Population health management is presented as a factor driving these organizational changes and as a mechanism to facilitate this change.

A focus on population health management, including the new strategies detailed earlier, is transforming and integrating the process of health care provision. This integration takes many forms, vertical and horizontal, between organizations, across disciplines, or within a single office. Accordingly, the volume is divided into four sections, presenting papers addressing transformation or integration of health care services (1) within health care organizations, (2) across health care organizations, and (3) between health care organizations and other fields such as local non-profits, health departments, and mental health and social services agencies; and (4) factors in PHM beyond the management of health care organizations.

SECTION I: PHM WITHIN HEALTH CARE ORGANIZATIONS

The first three papers in this volume address issues of PHM within health care organizations. PHM activities are frequently implemented in health care organizations under the umbrella of the patient-centered medical home (PCMH). The first paper, by Tahara and Green, positions the PCMH as a transformational organizational change because health care organizations must move to a team-based model of care as a radical departure from the current hierarchical medical practice model. The authors provide a concise review of the PCMH literature, and describe the challenges of implementation. They then propose tools from change management and systems thinking that health care leaders can employ to guide their organizations through the change process.

The second paper, by Hearld, Hearld, and Hogan, is a quantitative study of the association between community characteristics and the PCMH capacity within that community. The authors conducted a longitudinal analysis of data from more than a thousand ambulatory practices in Michigan participating in a large private insurer's incentive program. Employing linear growth curve models, the authors found distributional differences in PCMH resources across communities. Specifically, having high racial and socioeconomic diversity was associated with lower levels of PCMH capacity among primary care and specialty physician practices in that community. This study illustrates the potential influence of community factors on the population health management practices that occur within a single health care organization, in this case a private ambulatory practice. In the discussion, the authors raise questions about the ability of PCMHs to improve population health in vulnerable communities given the apparent nonrandom disparity in PCMH resources across communities.

The third chapter in this first section, by Moffatt-Bruce, McAlearney, Aldrich, Latimer, and Funai, is a case study of a health system-wide process improvement initiative. Within large health care systems, an important element of care management involves continuous monitoring and evaluation of quality of care, patient safety, and efficiency. A large Midwestern health system implemented Operations Councils in 15 units across the system; the goal was to utilize Lean process improvement techniques with frontline staff as trained Quality Improvement facilitators. The authors present results of positive changes in outcome metrics including improvements in area-specific and system-wide mortality and readmissions. The authors propose that in a large medical center, increased frontline staff engagement in patient safety initiatives improved process measures and patient outcomes, helping them to improve the health of the defined populations they serve.

SECTION II: PHM BETWEEN HEALTH CARE ORGANIZATIONS

Section II presents two case studies of PHM between health care organizations. In the paper titled "Using Teams to Implement Personalized Health Care across a Multi-Site Breast Cancer Network," Lewis, Bloom, Rice, Naeim, and Shortell explore organizational determinants of team effectiveness within the Athena Breast Health Network, a multi-site collaboration between five health systems. The authors employed a mixed methods analysis including key informant interviews and a multi-wave survey of team members at various levels across the five health systems. Their results reveal that group culture and supportive, collaborative environments are positively associated with team effectiveness, and a hierarchical culture is negatively associated with team effectiveness. When developing PHM collaborations between organizations, such as the one studied in this paper, organizational variables should be a focus of building a positive culture of inter-professional teamwork.

In the paper titled "A Business Planning Model to Identify New Safety Net Clinic Locations," Langabeer, Helton, DelliFraine, Dotson, Watts, and Love describe a community-based collaborative alliance of health care providers tasked with guiding decisions about expanding the community's network of community health clinics. This collaborative included stakeholders from 50 area health care organizations. Participants defined key variables including demand, sustainability, and competition and developed a mathematical decision model that used publicly available community data on these key variables to arrive at clinic locations. This collaborative followed a key tenant of PHM by using local, population-level data to guide health care planning. The authors propose that other communities can replicate this collaborative process to guide community health care planning decisions.

SECTION III: PHM INTEGRATING HEALTH CARE ORGANIZATIONS AND OTHER FIELDS

Section III includes three chapters that discuss issues of PHM between health care organizations and organizations in other fields. The paper titled "Answering the Call for Integrating Population Health: Insights from Health System Executives," by Carlton, explores the issues related to integrating health care and public health organizations for PHM activities. Qualitative analysis of key informant interviews with health system, health department, and non-profit executives identified strategies leaders might use to more effectively integrate these fields. The author proposes that health care executives can use these strategies to guide interactions and direct limited resources when developing PHM initiatives with public health departments and community organizations.

Sieck, Wickizer, and Geist, in the paper titled "Population Health Management in Integrated Physical and Mental Health Care," present a case study of integrating physical and mental health care for individuals with serious mental illness in the Missouri Health Home Program. The authors use PHM as a framework for integrating that care, highlighting particular elements of PHM that facilitate and support integration. As health care reform provides external motivation, this paper positions PHM as a guide for other states as they attempt to integrate physical and mental health care services.

The paper titled "Population, Community, and Public Health: Measuring the Benefits," by Turner and Evashwick, is a discussion of three related concepts, population health, community health, and public health. The authors define these three concepts and discuss current value metrics and measurement models for each. The proposed valuation techniques provide a framework for stakeholders to define, measure, and value initiatives under each of these concepts. Health care executives can use this paper as a guide to committing resources, assessing the potential of PHM initiatives, and determining models for evaluation of benefits.

SECTION IV: FACTORS IN PHM BEYOND THE MANAGEMENT OF HEALTH CARE ORGANIZATIONS

Section IV is a presentation of considerations in PHM beyond management strategies that leaders and scholars of health care organizations need to be aware of during the PHM implementation process. Section IV starts with an invited letter by Wexler, a practicing family physician, who calls us to consider the patient in the process of care transformation. Current policy presupposes that transformation of health care delivery will lead to patients proactively engaging in their own care, making healthy choices, and completing chronic disease self-management tasks. Wexler presents the results of a recent intervention to reduce non-urgent ED use among Medicaid patients in which a transformation of the process of care did not lead to a significant change in patient behavior. He proposes that effective PHM requires stakeholder acknowledgment of how non-health system factors affect patient behaviors and subsequently influence the success of PHM interventions.

In the final paper in this volume we outline current health care payment models and discusses the impact of each on the potential success of PHM initiatives. We then present the benefits of a multi-part model, combining visit-based fee-for-service reimbursement with a monthly "care coordination payment" and a performance-based payment system that recognizes achievement of quality and efficiency goals. This approach, however, is limited due to the current lack of standardized measurement of quality goals that are linked to payment incentives. As financial models dictated by health system payers are inextricably linked to the organization and management of health care, they indeed deserve comment in this volume.

We hope health care scholars and practitioners will find this volume of interest. It extends, we believe, our understanding of population health management efforts within and between health care organizations. The variety of studies and methods presented in this volume highlight the breadth of efforts currently underway to transform health care, and the potential for scholarship to advance the population health management agenda. In the first three sections of this volume we highlight the role for health care organizations and management in PHM. In the final section we provide a consideration of factors that can influence the success of health care redesign initiatives, specifically the voice and actions of the patient, and physician and hospital payment models. These issues should be considered by health care managers and scholars when implementing and evaluating PHM initiatives.

Jennifer L. Hefner
Timothy R. Huerta
Ann Scheck McAlearney
Editors

REFERENCES

Carman, K. L., Dardess, P., Maurer, M., Sofaer, S., Adams, K., Bechtel, C., & Sweeney, J. (2013). Patient and family engagement: A framework for understanding the elements and developing interventions and policies. *Health Affairs (Project Hope)*, *32*(2), 223–231. doi:10.1377/hlthaff.2012.1133.

Cusack, C. M., Knudson, A. D., Kronstadt, J. L., Singer, R. F., & Brown, A. L. (2010). *Practice-based population health: Information technology to support transformation to proactive primary care*. (No. 10-0092-EF). Rockville, MD: Agency for Healthcare Research and Quality.

Hacker, K., & Walker, D. K. (2013). Achieving population health in accountable care organizations. *American Journal of Public Health*, *103*(7), 1163–1167.

Halfon, N., & Conway, P. H. (2013). The opportunities and challenges of a lifelong health system. *The New England Journal of Medicine*, *368*(17), 1569–1571.

Huerta, T. R., Sieck, C. J., Hefner, J., Johansen, M., Wexler, R., & McAlearney, A. S. (2013). Patient centered care plus medical home does not equal patient centered medical home: Why layering models of care may not lead to better outcomes. *OA Family Medicine*, *1*(1), 5.

Magnan, S., Fisher, E., Kindig, D., Isham, G., Wood, D., Eustis, M., … Leitz, S. (2012). Achieving accountability for health and health care. *Minnesota Medicine*, *95*(11), 37–39.

McAlearney, A. (2003). *Population health management: Strategies to improve outcomes* (1st ed.). Chicago, IL: Health Administration Press.

McAlearney, A. S. (2002). Population health management in theory and practice. *Advances in health care management* (3rd ed., pp. 117–159). New York, NY: JAI Press.

McLellan, R. K., Sherman, B., Loeppke, R. R., McKenzie, J., Mueller, K. L., Yarborough, C. M., … Larson, P. W. (2012). Optimizing health care delivery by integrating workplaces, homes, and communities: How occupational and environmental medicine can serve as a vital connecting link between accountable care organizations and the patient-centered medical home. *Journal of Occupational and Environmental Medicine/American College of Occupational and Environmental Medicine*, *54*(4), 504–512.

Parton, R., & Ravi, S. (2012). ACO rule has big implications for IT. New population health tools needed to effectively manage ACOs. *Health Management Technology*, *33*(4), 12–14.

SECTION I
PHM WITHIN HEALTH CARE ORGANIZATIONS

STRATEGIC RE-DESIGN OF TEAM-BASED PATIENT-FOCUSED HEALTH CARE SERVICES

Denise C. Tahara and Richard P. Green

ABSTRACT

Purpose – *This paper proposes an organizational change process to prepare physicians and other health professionals for their new roles in patient-centered medical homes (PCMHs). It provides physician-centered tools, models, concepts, and the language to implement transformational patient-centered medical care.*

Design/methodology/approach – *To improve care delivery, quality, and patient engagement, a systems approach to care is required. This paper examines a systems approach to patient care where all inputs that influence patient interactions and participation are considered in the design of health care delivery and follow-up treatment plans. Applying systems thinking, organizational change models, and team-building, we have examined the continuum of this change process from ideation through the diffusion of new methods and behaviors.*

Findings – *PCMHs make compelling business sense. Studies have shown that the PCMH improves patient satisfaction, clinical outcomes*

Population Health Management in Health Care Organizations
Advances in Health Care Management, Volume 16, 3–22

ISSN: 1474-8231/doi:10.1108/S1474-823120140000016000

and reduces underuse and overuse of medical services. Patient-centered care necessitates transitioning from an adversarial to a collaborative culture. It is a transformation process predicated on strong leadership able to align an organization toward a vision of patient-centered care, creating a collaborative culture committed to health-goal achievement.

Originality/value – *This paper proposes that the PCMH is a rigorous team-building transformational organizational change, a radical departure from the current hierarchical, silo-oriented, medical practice model. It requires that participants within and across health care organizations learn new skills and behaviors to achieve the anticipated quality and efficiency improvements. It is an innovative health care organization model of the future whose success is premised on teams supplanting the individual as the building block and unit of health care performance.*

Keywords: Patient-centered medical home; team-based health care; strategic design; systems thinking; organizational transformation; leadership development

INTRODUCTION

A recent international study of health care systems by the Commonwealth Fund determined that patients with complex care needs who received health care through a coordinated care model such as a patient-centered medical care model had better health outcomes than those who navigated the health care systems themselves. There was better communication among providers, and sharing of patient data and costs were less (Schoen et al., 2011). These results are significant as we mark the birth of the seven billionth person and our global communities seek new ways to provide care to an increasing and aging population, and simultaneously decrease overall costs.

The survey concluded that in all 11 countries, coordinating care for *all* patients is needed. Therefore, the delivery of health care services must be transformed. Health care needs to be strategically designed around patient-provider teams and the larger care community, including families and local neighborhoods. All of these stakeholders need to collaborate toward achieving the goal of improved population health and wellbeing. This paper will explore this process.

Although we see improvements in efficiency and effectiveness of health care across the globe, in the United States (US), we still struggle to improve health care access and delivery. For example, in the same study, 42% of those surveyed in the US reported not visiting a doctor, filling a prescription, or getting recommended care. Moreover, the US ranks last among the industrialized countries in "mortality amenable to healthcare" that are caused by partially preventable or treatable conditions such as ischemic heart disease, diabetes, stroke, and bacterial infections (The Commonwealth Fund, 2011).

The patient-centered medical home (PCMH) is a rigorous team-based transformational organizational change initiative that provides coordinated, continuous patient-centric medical care, managed by a team of individuals led by a physician and is an alternative approach to current health care delivery systems. Driving the development of this collaborative delivery of health care is a considerable body of research on the impact of primary care-oriented health care systems on patient health outcomes, costs, and equity. Despite recognition of the importance of patient-centered care and evidence of its effectiveness, our health care system falls short of implementing it (American Hospital Association, 2010). The core belief of this model is that enhanced support for primary care will lead to improved quality, increased access and reduced health care costs (Baron, 2009).

PATIENT-CENTERED MEDICAL HOMES

Patient centeredness refers to health care that establishes a partnership among practitioners, patients, and their families to ensure that decisions respect patients' wants, needs, and preferences and that patients have the education and support they require to make decisions and participate in their own care (Institute of Medicine, 2001, p. 7).

Notwithstanding advocacy for this new organizing framework, our health care system remains fragmented, hierarchical, and silo-oriented. It is a medical practice model that does not encourage utilization, coordination, continuity and communication across health care settings. We propose that the patient-centered medical care model can significantly improve the quality and efficiency of patient care through improved partnerships and economical, clinically aligned relationships.

The promise of PCMHs is comprehensive care coordination where there is centralization and communication of patient data to improve quality, appropriateness, efficiency, and overall health of the patient. The PCMH was developed to address socio-economic barriers to care by providing patients with a usual source of care including preventive and wellness care. The Joint Commission's refocus on patient flow highlights the current crowding in the ED which continues to increase at an unsustainable rate (Calloway, 2012). Increased utilization of primary care services results in decreased hospitalizations and ED use. Typical PCMHs segment the market by age and then by gender. This enables them to focus on whole patient care, by planning and coordinating services and activities both within and outside the health care setting, aimed at addressing lifestyle behaviors and practices to improve health and wellness.

In the 2011 Commonwealth survey, patients with medical homes (in all 11 countries) reported better care experiences than those without medical homes. Further, patients reported fewer coordination failures with their care, including medical errors and duplicate testing. They also had better follow-up care post hospitalization and better discharge planning (Schoen et al., 2011). Much of this is attributed to the strong relationships developed with the primary care physicians (PCPs), a hallmark of the PCMH model of care.

Electronic medical records (EMRs) are central to improving communication among providers within and across settings as well as to decreasing overall health care costs. Successful PCMHs utilize health information technology to facilitate clinical decision making and improve utilization of services. From the patient's perspective, they capture and centralize patient information – there is two-way communication. From the provider's perspective, timely information regarding patient history, medication lists, and treatment notes can decrease duplicate testing and overuse of other diagnostic and ancillary health care services, to reduce costs, reduce errors, and improve clinical decision making and patient safety.

THE CHALLENGE

Change has always been a significant leadership challenge, even change referred to as normal or falling within the scope of existing leadership approaches. The PCMH is a major change to care delivery that requires people at all levels within the health care system to learn new behaviors and skills. "For most primary care practices, the development of effective teams that are true drivers of care integration would be the greatest departure from the status quo" (Porter, Pabo, & Lee, 2013, p. 519). This is a much more difficult challenge. This is a system transformed, asking providers to step into the patient's shoes and perhaps for the first time, as part of diagnosis and treatment, to consider their patient's cultural traditions, personal preferences, values, built environment and lifestyles. Patients are considered to be an important part of the health care team, expected to work collaboratively and make decisions with their providers, taking a life-course perspective.

For most clinical practices, the transformation process to a PCMH model can be extremely complicated and stressful. Care delivery continues to be fragmented, patients are many times disengaged or disenfranchised; there is a lack of transparency and there is little interoperability of EMRs across institutional and system settings.

As practices adopt the PCMH model, many maintain their existing structures, silos, and hierarchies. We see collaboration among the nonclinical staff organized around physicians, their schedules and delivery needs, reinforcing social and cultural barriers. Many health care organizations do not recognize or support interdisciplinary teams and teamwork (Chesluk & Holmboe, 2010). Health care professionals are trained separately and not taught how to work as part of interprofessional teams. There is much offloading of tasks; roles and responsibilities are not clearly defined including overall coordination of services and assignment of that responsibility. This results in tremendous waste of resources as clinical staff perform tasks below their skill and training and therefore are not available to perform the tasks that they have the expertise to do. This can be improved through better alignment of care and expertise, "where team members work at their highest level [versus lowest] of expertise in a coordinated effort to achieve common goals" (Berry & Mirabito, 2010, p. 163).

The transformation process requires strong leadership aligned with the objectives of the organization and who understand the requirements for success including the capacity for organizational learning and development – because in most cases, culture change is essential. The current silos that exist within the clinical specializations must be eliminated and the locus of control needs to reside with the patient and their family. For successful transformation to patient-centered care models, health leaders need the knowledge and tools to guide this process. The first step is understanding the current system and identifying the requisite improvements to be made that will facilitate patients traversing their care from multiple providers across multiple settings. A strong guiding coalition to lead the change process and manage the patient's health is needed.

TRANSFORMING TO A TEAM-BASED APPROACH AND APPLYING SYSTEMS THINKING

For new models of care to provide value to all stakeholders in the system, leadership must reimagine the care delivery process. What are the key process variables and key quality characteristics that attract our patients to our system? How do we deliver on these variables? To improve care delivery, quality and patient engagement, a systems approach to care is required where all inputs that influence patient interactions and participation are considered in the design of health care delivery and follow-up treatment plans. Patient-centered care requires a team of professionals coordinating care that addresses the individual needs of the patients. Managers must look beyond the dominant acute care model, where innovation means adding on services and capabilities instead of identifying those components that will improve care delivery, efficiency, effectiveness, and health outcomes.

As we consider new models of patient-centered care, we need to shift our approach from an encounter-based or episodic care to a life-course approach which must be designed in to the system, before the patient's first encounter. Our approach to care must shift toward primary care and prevention, to keep patients healthy and out of the ED. Systems are optimized when the benefits are maximized to all participants (Tahara, 2014). Physician leaders must understand the current landscape of the operating environment from two systems' perspectives: from the patient's experience as presented in Fig. 1, and also from the providers' perspective, to evaluate the delivery system and identify ways to improve the transitions within and across health care systems (Fig. 2).

More importantly, as providers we must direct patients to the appropriate point of entry into the health care system. Root cause analysis is a useful tool to identify the barriers, challenges, and facilitators to appropriate access to and utilization of the system. The factors that drive care choices can be organized into the following categories: Social, Environmental, Economic and Provider, as represented in Fig. 3.

These systems tools provide visual representations of the current delivery systems. They are best used as communication tools for performance improvement. For multidisciplinary teams they are particularly useful to discuss and identify the key inputs, processes, and desired outcomes from health care delivery. Using reverse logic, by starting with the desired outcome of improved population wellness and wellbeing, we can assess how we perform on the characteristics and variables identified as important to the patient. We can then evaluate the experience from the patient's

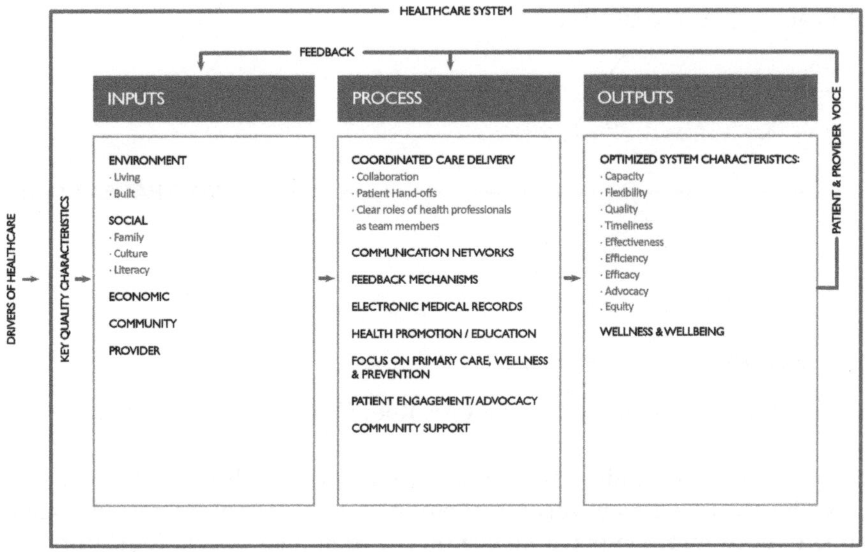

Fig. 1. Health Care Delivery Process.

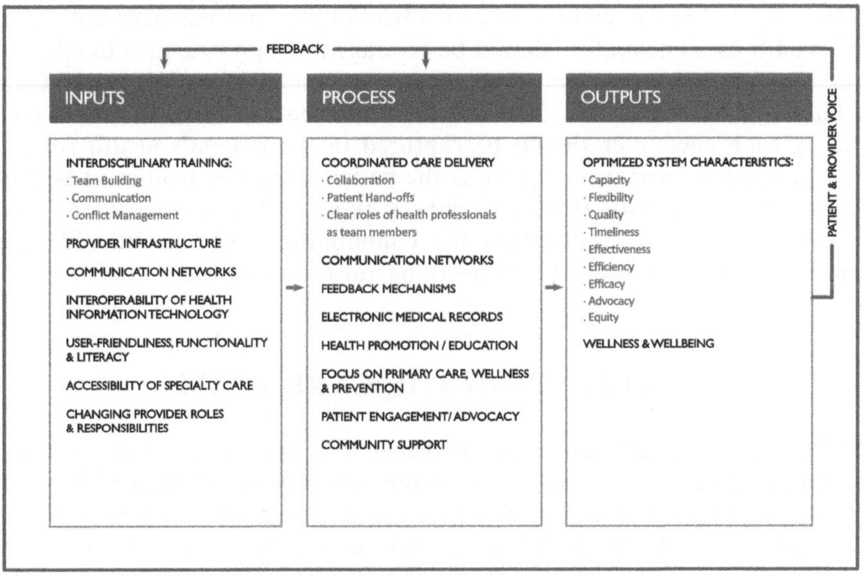

Fig. 2. Provider Care Coordination Process.

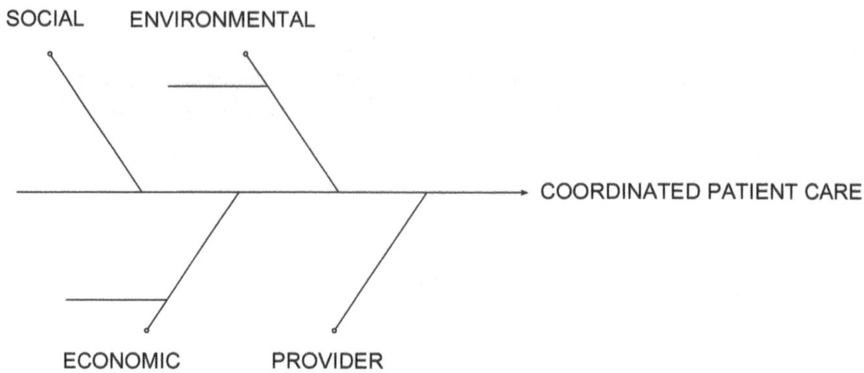

Fig. 3. Coordinated Patient Care Root Cause Analysis Template.

perspective; better understanding how they navigate through the care process. We then feed back this information to inform the process and determine how to improve performance on the identified system indicators. To do this, we must build in opportunities for the patient to provide feedback on their experience: the challenges, barriers, and facilitators to adhering to care plans and treatment protocols. This is especially important for patient follow-up if they are to be active members of the care management team. All health care encounters should be leveraged as opportunities to educate and reinforce wellness and wellbeing and empower patients and their families (Tahara & Laufer, 2014). Patient information collected and shared during each encounter should be captured in the patient's health record. For example, information regarding the patient's environment must be collected and shared with all team members; those within and across the providers' systems and also within the community, where healthy lifestyle choices can be supported. The transitions must be seamless.

CATALYZING THE CARE TEAM

PCMH is a more difficult change challenge that cannot be met through the current medical-model, top-down, command-and-control leadership style. Because behavioral change occurs more readily and enthusiastically in and through teams, change of this scale depends on the work of teams. New models of care will require that physicians take a proactive approach to managing patients' health and wellness, collaboratively. Physicians will need to coordinate services and deliver care where they will have a different role, responsibilities and accountability; teams will not be organized vertically around the physician, but rather horizontally around the patient's needs. Physician training will need to include new communication and leadership skills such as shared decision making, power and authority, and conflict resolution, to better manage the whole patient, in some cases with multiple diseases.

It is important to have a guiding coalition to champion the effort including new and innovative approaches to care delivery (MacPhee, Wardrop, & Campbell, 2010). The collective commitment of teams keeps members from feeling threatened by change as individuals left to defend themselves against ambiguity and suspicion; they need to be part of the change process. Teams can make the hierarchy response without weakening, energize across boundaries without distorting them, and can entertain many perspectives without undermining or refuting. As an organizational model of the future, that is, networked, nonhierarchical, horizontal, PCMH will be premised on the team, surpassing the individual as a building block and unit of performance.

Katzenbach and Smith (2005) suggest a number of practices shared by successful teams that can be utilized to navigate the white water of patient-centered medical care transformation. These include:

1. *Establish urgency, demanding performance standards, and direction.* Transitioning to a PCMH model or other collaborative care model can be the needed catalyst for total system transformation. Buy-in to a new system of care delivery will be easier starting with team-based care. All members of the PCMH team, including family physicians, internal medicine specialists, nurse practitioners, other clinicians, need to believe that they are contributing to a worthwhile and urgent process of managing patient health and wellbeing. The more urgent and meaningful the rationale for the PCMH, the more likely the health care team will meet or exceed its performance standards.
2. *Select members for skill and skill potential, not personality.* No PCMH will survive without the skill needed to provide continuous and comprehensive health care. Adding people with varied skills and knowledge to the team increases the number of possible solutions that will be generated to improve health outcomes. The majority of knowledge-sharing and innovation is through people interacting with people within networks, groups, or teams that cross conventional organizational boundaries. It is essential that all teams have the requisite skill sets to deliver quality care using the new approach.

3. *Pay attention to first meetings and actions*. Initial impressions always mean a great deal. The PCP leads a team of individuals who take responsibility for ongoing care of patients. What the personal physician pays attention to, how s/he does it, and when is probably more important than what s/he says. Trust in health care delivery has declined at an alarming rate, with the confidence in leaders of medical institutions declining from 73% in 1966 to 32% in 2004. Contributing to this low sense of trust is an overemphasis on profits, the unscrupulous behavior of large health care providers, and the bias of negative reporting on a troubled and challenged health care system (Shore, as cited in Mathis, 2006). Improved care quality does not mean a decrease in profitability.
4. *Set clear rules of behavior*. Teams will have to develop explicit strategies, systems and health objectives to ensure clarity of roles and routines, and how the members contribute to sustained working relationships. All effective teams develop rules of conduct that smooth the process of purpose to performance. Rules hold members accountable for patient outcomes, team performance, communications, confidentiality, diagnostic approach, conflict management, and work contributions. Roles and responsibilities should be clearly defined. Establishing a schedule of team meetings provides a mechanism to communicate information vital to patient care. This is especially important when team members are dispersed across institutions versus colocated in the same facility. Communication involves frequent and informal face-to-face contact with all organizational members and members of the coalition, as well as implementing processes and behaviors that communicate the commitment to the shared vision. In other words, walk the talk. Create feedback loops that will continue to inform the system.
5. *Challenge PCMH members regularly with fresh facts and information*. Effective team membership will require feedback that informs practices and team members about the outcome of their personal and collective behavior, patient health, and resource utilization. Mandatory process and system measures should be benchmarked and monitored for opportunities for improvement or sharing of successful practices. While patient confidentiality is paramount, sharing of patient information is essential to clinical decision making and comprehensive patient management. Data regarding patient handoffs, acute and emergent episodes, medication lists, diagnostic tests, and treatment notes must be available to clinical team members. EMRs across institutional settings are essential.

As we review the members of patient care teams, we should consider stakeholders who should play a larger role in the decision making and management of the health of the whole patient, including the patient themselves, family members, pharmacists, and community members since much of patient health care occurs outside institutional settings. Health care planning requires a public health, community-focused strategy where transportation, translation, environmental, food security, and workplace safety factors are considered; since much of the management of health and wellbeing requires lifestyle behavioral changes, follow-up care, routines and regimens at home, including diet and exercise. This requires active patient engagement and participation from family and communities. Patient centeredness requires collaboration among health care and non-health care providers including community resources such as public health and social services. Care is truly designed around the patient's needs as illustrated in Fig. 4.

The key to successful health outcomes and improved wellbeing is patient engagement. Patients who are engaged in their care report better care experiences, have better health outcomes, and lower costs (Lesser, Fineberg, & Cassel, 2010; Schoen et al., 2011). Even though the medical home model is designed to be patient centered, many times this does not mean patient friendly and frequently, patients are left to navigate the

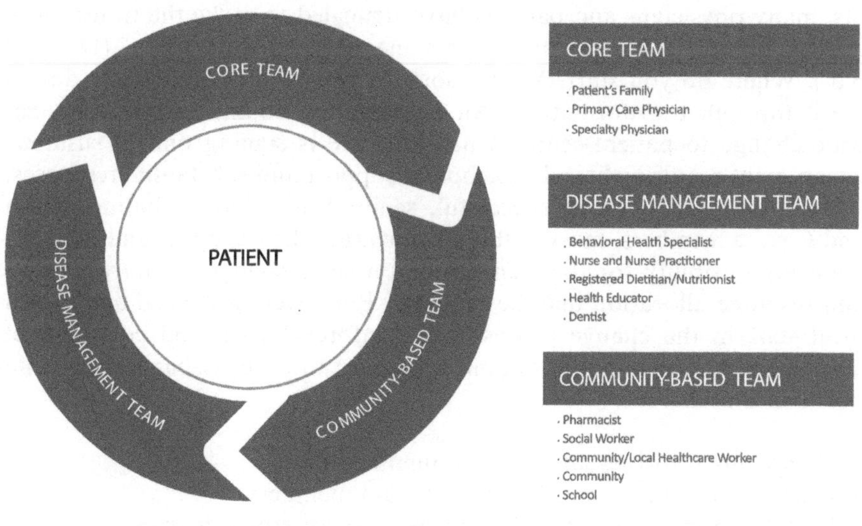

Fig. 4. Patient-Centered Care and Management. *Source*: Tahara and Laufer (2014).

complex system of care by themselves. Although the PCMH model encourages integration of treatment and services, we find that much of that coordination occurs within "integrated" systems and not across health care settings or continuum of care. Further, although the patients have a single point of entry to the health care system, it does not guarantee the required accountability for patient management, especially with regard to medication management, care transitions and coverage.

"Designing innovations and treatment plans, must move the patient from awareness to actualization of their care, facilitate success and engage them in their health and well-being. Designing the patient experience and leveraging the positive and prosocial effects of media is essential for compliance and participation" (American Academy of Pediatrics, 2013; Tahara & Laufer, 2014). We must engage our patients using communication mechanisms and media familiar to them; they need to feel confident and competent.

THE PROCESS

Wide-scale adoption of the PCMH model would represent a fundamental change from the current system of delivering patient care. Despite the benefits, many physicians and patients have struggled to make the transition to medical homes. "Change starts when someone sees the next step" (Drayton, n.d.). Where do you start? With whom do you get involved? How do you see it through transformation? An organization committing to a system-wide change to patient-centered medical care is signing onto a sustained engagement requiring broad stakeholder support and substantial resources.

For this process to be successful, senior leadership, including clinical and C-suite members, must visibly demonstrate their support and take ultimate responsibility for the transformation since changes in infrastructure and resource allocation may be required. Empowering clinical and nonclinical staff in the change process will reinforce buy-in and commitment. This support is essential if organizations are to address barriers to collaboration that include:

- Competing priorities and goal misalignment;
- Unclear roles and responsibilities of team members;
- Lack of performance metrics to measure successful outcomes;
- Resource constraints and misalignment; and
- Inadequate system design to support new methods of care delivery.

Once these system challenges have been identified, cross-functional teams from within the organization and external to the organization should work together to re-design the service experience and the delivery process identifying innovative ways to perform tasks and deliver coordinated care. PCMH care teams are organized around individual patient needs and health conditions. Care teams need to work collaboratively across departments and settings, sharing the management and control over patient care. This model is a significant departure from current medical models organized around specialty or disease versus around treating the whole patient. Care delivery must reinforce the patient focused, shared-clinical decision making to improve health outcomes and transformation to a PCMH practice.

Health care leaders need to get better at convincing people that we are facing an acute problem at the systems level and immediate action is required. In health care, providers understand the immediacy of the problem. To develop a sense of urgency around the need for change requires a broad internal dialogue regarding the current delivery of health care. This should include management skills and leadership style assessments, scenario analysis, root cause analysis, case reviews, and use of strategic planning tools with a wide cross-section of all relevant stakeholders participating in the process. The PCMH is a completely different model of managing patient care. Further, at the patient level, this will require commitment from all team members toward achieving agreed-upon health objectives and ensuring that these services are coordinated.

A drive for change without a clear focus will rapidly fizzle unless leadership develops a clear vision of the future to direct the change effort. That future must be accompanied by a clear description about new practice patterns and collaboration to improve health and wellness, decrease costs, ensure appropriate utilization of constrained resources and be sustainable. The vision needs to be defined in such a way that it is capable of communication in a short "vision speech" or sound bite that conveys the heart of the change in less than five minutes and is recapped in a powerful one- or two-sentence summary. All team members need to be fluent in the vision statement and develop the strategies that will deliver the vision.

Health care leaders will need opportunities to practice implementing and testing these new approaches to care. They need practice fields to engage them in decision-making opportunities, to use new skills, tools, frameworks, and feedback. Training opportunities should be created for health care professionals to evaluate their behavior in teams, practice shared decision making, and changing roles, where they may transition from team leader to a team member over the life course of the patient. How physicians are perceived by their patients effects the patients' confidence and trust in their care. Communication and interactions among team members will also effect the trust of the patient and their adherence to treatment protocols.

LEADERSHIP DEVELOPMENT

The current approaches to leadership development are not suited to developing health care leaders who can engage in collaborative processes and are capable of aligning a myriad of talents toward a vision of patient-centered care. Leadership development, historically associated with developing leaders as heroes, is being transformed to a leadership model extolling collective and collaborative effort toward a committed purpose. Leadership development programs must reflect the realistic challenges that leaders will face if they are to be fully prepared to enter the white water of large-scale health care transformation.

A collaborative leadership model is something people do together, acknowledging the benefit of diversity, sharing information, and leveraging collective decision making. It is a very different model of leadership from that of one actor as the lone determinant of transformation. Leadership is now an interdependent set of relationships among leaders and followers who understand and mutually agree on a purpose (Rost, 1993).

Simulations, or microworlds, are a way leaders can begin to investigate and develop trust in new models of leadership and the principles of a collaborative, team-based health care system. They are not about remembering a process or set of procedures that provide practitioners with a formalized resolution to a problem. Simulations create a practice field where the concomitant behavioral processes associated with problem finding and resolution, promoting agendas and influencing others can be explored and discussed in a real-world scenario. Organizations need an opportunity to practice what they preach; simulation provides an opportunity for health-care providers to practice a new model of collaborative leadership (Keys, Fulmer, & Stumpf, 1996).

Rather than learning vicariously through the game-based analytics of computer simulations or the consultant-like behaviors encouraged by case study, a behavioral simulation is an interactive experience with an emphasis on experiential learning. Behavioral simulations highlight the interpersonal dynamics between people as they individually and collectively grapple with volatile, risky, continually changing environments (Keys et al., 1996).

Roles in a behavioral simulation are connected through both extensive background information and current information as provided through e-mails, attachments, and reports, helping to create interpersonal dynamics and the reality of the organization. With the continuing push for information, there is a need for good communication skills, to set priorities, the ability to manage conflict around scarce resources, as participants are likely to behave as they do in their "real" world; they pay attention to some issues and filter out others to be left unaddressed (Dunbar, Stumpf, Mullen, & Arnone, 1992).

Trained simulation facilitators observe the simulation and guide the process through which participants share information and come to better understand their management style and behaviors. Behavioral simulations are excellent team-building and skill-building vehicles; they generate feedback about organizational process and also provide an opportunity for feedback about the participant's individual skills and their effectiveness (Keys et al., 1996).

Simulations are even more powerful when linked through the use of tools and well-designed activities intended to influence personal mindset-shift, capability, and organizational alignment. The personal style participants use to influence decisions is in part based on their personality and preferences, distinct from skills and competencies. Individual styles can have a profound impact on the way managers and leaders grapple with organizational complexity, manage subunit rivalry, balance ambiguity, and stay on track despite a plethora of distraction.

The *Myers-Briggs Type Indicator (MBTI)* is a research-based questionnaire used to measure how people take in information and make decisions. First published in 1962, the questionnaire identifies 16 different personality types. Teams are most effective when they understand and value the different preferences of their members. The nuances of differences may distract people from collaboration and shifting thinking can help create a well-rounded, more productive team. The MBTI is predicated on the premise that teams consist of people who have unique gifts and talents, as well as challenges and obstacles to overcome and gives participants an opportunity to apply knowledge and skills to fill the gap (Dunbar et al., 1992).

The *Fundamental Interpersonal Relations Orientation-Behavior (FIRO-B)* instrument was created in the late 1950s to help understand and predict how high performance teams might work together. The instrument helps people better understand their personal needs and how those needs influence their communication and personal style. The FIRO-B measures behaviors influenced by personal needs for social interactions and associations, control or influence over others, preference to be led and influenced, as well as the need to build relationships with others. The FIRO-B can be used in conjunction with the MBTI instrument to accelerate team-building and help team members overcome barriers to success and higher levels of performance (Schnell & Hammer, 2004) (Fig. 5).

Stakeholder Analysis is the process of identifying and sorting individuals or groups likely to influence or be influenced by the team outcomes. The purpose of stakeholder analysis is to better anticipate the influence that these individuals or groups will have on team performance and to help develop strategies to influence support and reduce obstacles to team success. W-Cubed is a diagnostic heuristic posing a series of questions: What do we want? What do they want? What can we do together? It was designed to gain insight into how individuals and team members can act more effectively. The answers guide behaviors similar to a physician's diagnostic questions which might help to guide their diagnosis and prescription. Stakeholder analysis does not obligate satisfaction of these stakeholders; it does identify issues of mutual benefit and issues that might be best avoided (Stumpf & Mullen, 1992).

NEXT STEPS

With the passage of the Patient Protection and Affordable Care Act, health care leadership must organize their systems to accommodate

	INCLUSION	CONTROL	AFFECTION
EXPRESSED BEHAVIOR "I make efforts to ..."	I make efforts to include other people in my activities and to get them to include me in theirs. I try to belong, to join social groups, and to be with people as much as possible.	I try to exert control and influence over things. I take charge of things and tell other people what to do.	I make efforts to become close to people. I express friendly and affectionate feelings and try to be personal and intimate.
WANTED BEHAVIOR " I want other people to..."	I want other people to include me in their activities and to invite me to belong, even if I do not make an effort to be included.	I want others to control and influence me. I want other people to tell me what to do.	I want others to express friendly and affectionate feelings toward me and try to become close to me.

Fig. 5. FIRO-B (Fundamental Interpersonal Relations Orientation-Behavior) Assessment Tool. *Source*: Schutz (1958). Retrieved from: http://www.primarygoals.org/diagrams/firo-b-schutz/

increased utilization and manage issues of equity and resource constraints. Creative solutions for supplemental capacity must be developed as part of new models of care delivery. Stakeholders must be engaged in the health care process. By defining the current challenges in the operating environment we can then focus on coordinating wellness care and prevention, chronic disease management, and acute health episodes. Every patient interaction should be viewed as an opportunity to improve health and wellbeing. The focus cannot be only on the chief complaint, but on the whole patient – understanding the needs of the patient versus focusing on the disease (Saha, Beach, & Cooper, 2008).

The Patient Protection and Affordable Care Act provides an opportunity for widespread implementation of innovations in care delivery designed to improve health outcomes. These opportunities exist however, in a fragmented, dysfunctional health care system that does not support the required access, coordination, continuity, and communication of health care across settings. The PCMH model in its concept and in practice is a significant departure from the hierarchical, silo-oriented medical practice models currently in place. Team members are vested and committed to health-goal achievement. Patient centeredness depends on activated, engaged patients who want better service and transparency in health care and seek to form partnerships with health care practices (Nutting et al., 2011).

PCMHs make compelling business sense. Studies have shown that the PCMH improves patient satisfaction, clinical outcomes and reduces underuse and overuse of medical services. Transformation to a patient-centered model requires innovative, out-of-the-box thinking and will re-design our entire health care delivery system. Such a collaborative team-building approach leverages the competencies and capabilities from multiple health care providers to improve patient health and wellbeing. Engagement of patients in their care decision making will encourage follow-up care and healthy lifestyle behaviors that are consistent with agreed-upon health objectives. This results in decreased costs and improved long-term health of individuals and communities. In 2008, the World Health Organization Commission on Social Determinants of Health reported that, "communities and cities that ensure access to basic goods, that are socially cohesive, that are designed to promote good physical and psychological wellbeing and that are protective of the natural environment are essential for health equity" (as cited in Friel et al., 2011, p. 863).

New more inclusive models of care will require that physicians coordinate and collaborate through an unchartered landscape of different roles, responsibilities, and accountability. Care teams must be developed around patient life-course needs, engaging them in managing their health and wellness and being mindful of critical patient handoffs. The key to any patient management system is planning and coordination of care, and communication of relevant health care information among all members of the care team, thereby improving decision making and health outcomes. There must be mutual respect and trust among all team members. Information technology and reimbursement systems must be redesigned to facilitate achieving the goals of improved health outcomes and decreased costs. To engage patients in their care, health information technology should be integrated into their care plan and facilitate adherence to treatment protocols and support decision making. To improve utilization of the technology, it must be familiar to the patient and a medium in which the patient feels competent and confident of the design.

A systems approach to care delivery will be required to effectively evaluate inputs to care inclusive of the patient's experience, their challenges and barriers in seeking care, adherence to treatment plans, and the traverse across providers. This new model of care requires feedback mechanisms to inform providers of the patient's built and living environments affecting their health and wellness.

Physician training will need to include new skills and competencies including improved listening skills as team members versus team leaders, to effectively help physicians facilitate patient care that not only treats disease, but also recognizes and encourages patients as stakeholders in their health care delivery. Collaborative models of education and interprofessional training should be designed into the transformation process. Metrics for patient satisfaction should include indicators that reflect collaboration and coordination among providers, particularly as more institutions are reimbursed using value-based purchasing models.

Patient-centered care necessitates transitioning from an adversarial to a collaborative culture. It requires that participants within and across health care organizations learn new skills and behaviors to achieve the anticipated quality and efficiency improvements. It is a transformation process predicated on strong leadership able to align an organization toward a vision of patient-centered care, creating a collaborative culture committed to health-goal achievement.

REFERENCES

American Academy of Pediatrics. (2013). *Policy statement: Children, adolescents, and the media*. Retrieved from www.pediatrics.org/dgi/doi/10.1542/peds.2013-2356

American Hospital Association. (2010). *Patient centered medical home.* AHA Research Synthesis Report. Retrieved from http://www.aha.org/research/cor/patient-centered/index.shtml

Baron, R. J. (2009). The chasm between intention and achievement in primary care. *Journal of the American Medical Association, 301*(18), 1922–1923.

Berry, L. L., & Mirabito, A. M. (2010). Innovative healthcare delivery. *Business Horizons, 53,* 157–169.

Calloway, S. D. (2012). *The joint commission's new patient flow standards.* Retrieved from http://urgentmatters.org/e-newsletter/current_issue/innovations_9.3

Chesluk, B. J., & Holmboe, E. S. (2010). How teams work or don't in primary care: A field study on internal medicine practices. *Health Affairs, 29*(5), 874–879.

Drayton, W. (n.d.). *ThinkExist.com Quotations Online.* Retrieved from http://en.thinkexist.com/quotes/William_Drayton/. Accessed on October 1, 2011.

Dunbar, R. L. M., Stumpf, S. A., Mullen, T. P., & Arnone, M. (1992). Management development: Choosing the right leadership simulation for the task. *Journal of Management Education, 16,* 220.

Friel, S., Akerman, M., Hancock, T., Kumaresan, J., Marmot, M., Melin, T., & Vlahov, D. (2011). Addressing the social and environmental determinants of urban health equity: Evidence for action and a research agenda. *Journal of Urban Health, 88*(5), 860–874.

Institute of Medicine: Hurtado, M.P., Swift, E. K., & Corrigan, J. (2001). *Envisioning a national health care quality report.* Washington, D.C.: National Academy Press.

Katzenbach, J. R., & Smith, D. K. (2005). The discipline of teams. *Harvard Business Review. 83*(7), 162–171.

Keys, J. B., Fulmer, R. M., & Stumpf, S.A. (1996). Microworlds and simuworlds: Practice fields for the learning organization. *Organizational Dynamics, 24*(4), 36–49.

Lesser, C. S., Fineberg, H. V., & Cassel, C. K. (2010). Physician payment reform: Principles that should shape. *Health Affairs, 29*(5), 948–952.

MacPhee, M., Wardrop, A., & Campbell, C. (2010). Transforming work place relationships through share decision making. *Journal of Nursing Management, 18,* 1016–1026.

Mathis, R. S. (2006). The trust prescription for healthcare: Building your reputation with consumers. *Journal of Medical Ethics, 32*(9), 565–566. Retrieved from http://www.ncbi.nlm.nih.gov/pmc/articles/PMC2563410/?tool=pmcentrez

Nutting, P. A., Crabtree, B. F., Miller, W. L., Stange, K. C., Stewart, E., & Jaen, C. (2011). Transforming physician practices to patient-centered medical homes: Lessons from the national demonstration project. *Health Affairs, 30*(3), 439–445.

Porter, M. E., Pabo, E. A., & Lee, T. H. (2013). Redesigning primary care: A strategic vision to improve value by organizing around patients' needs. *Health Affairs, 32*(3), 516–525.

Rost, J. C. (1993). Leadership development in the new millennium. *Journal of Leadership Studies, 1*(1), 90–110.

Saha, S., Beach, M. C., & Cooper, L. A. (2008). Patient centeredness, cultural competence and healthcare quality. *Journal of National Medical Association, 100*(11), 1275–1285.

Schnell, E. R., & Hammer, A. L. (2004). *Introduction to the FIRO-B instrument in organizations.* Palo Alto, CA: Consulting Psychologists Press.

Schoen, C., Osborn, R., Squires, D., Doty, M., Pierson, R., & Applebaum, A. (2011). New 2011 survey of patients with complex care needs in eleven countries finds that care is often poorly coordinated. *Health Affairs, 30*(12), 2437–2448. Retrieved from http://www.commonwealthfund.org/Publications/In-the-Literature/2011/Nov/2011-International-Survey-Of-Patients.aspx

Schutz, W. (1958). *Fundamental Interpersonal Relations Orientation-Behavior (FIRO-B) assessment*. Retrieved from http://www.primarygoals.org/diagrams/firo-b-schutz/

Stumpf, S. A., & Mullen, T. P. (1992). *Taking charge: Strategic leadership in the middle game*. Upper Saddle River, NJ: Prentice Hall.

Tahara, D. (2014). A life course approach to family-centered care: Improving pediatric health and well-being. In S. S. Jhangiani & J. Wylie-Rosett (Eds.), *Obesity & Disease in an Inter-Connected World: A Systems Approach to Turn Huge Challenges into Amazing Opportunities*. Oak Park, IL: Bentham Science.

Tahara, D., & Laufer, G. (2014). From intervention to innovation: Health information technology. In S. S. Jhangiani & J. Wylie-Rosett (Eds.), *Obesity & Disease in an Inter-Connected World: A Systems Approach to Turn Huge Challenges into Amazing Opportunities*. Oak Park, IL: Bentham Science.

The Commonwealth Fund. (2011). *Why not the best? Results from the National Scorecard on US Health System Performance, 2011*. Retrieved from http://www.commonwealthfund.org/Publications/Fund-Reports/2011/Oct/Why-Not-the-Best-2011.aspx

COMMUNITY-LEVEL SOCIODEMOGRAPHIC CHARACTERISTICS AND PATIENT-CENTERED MEDICAL HOME CAPACITY

Larry R. Hearld, Kristine R. Hearld and Tory H. Hogan

ABSTRACT

Purpose – *Longitudinally (2008–2012) assess whether community-level sociodemographic characteristics were associated with patient-centered medical home (PCMH) capacity among primary care and specialty physician practices, and the extent to which variation in PCMH capacity can be accounted for by sociodemographic characteristics of the community.*

Design/methodology/approach – *Linear growth curve models among 523 small and medium-sized physician practices that were members of a consortium of physician organizations pursuing the PCMH.*

Population Health Management in Health Care Organizations
Advances in Health Care Management, Volume 16, 23–50

ISSN: 1474-8231/doi:10.1108/S1474-823120140000016002

Findings – *Our analysis indicated that the average level of sociodemographic characteristics was typically not associated with the level of PCMH capacity, but the heterogeneity of the surrounding community is generally associated with lower levels of capacity. Furthermore, these relationships differed for interpersonal and technical dimensions of the PCMH.*

Implications – *Our findings suggest that PCMH capabilities may not be evenly distributed across communities and raise questions about whether such distributional differences influence the PCMH's ability to improve population health, especially the health of vulnerable populations. Such nuances highlight the challenges faced by practitioners and policy makers who advocate the continued expansion of the PCMH as a means of improving the health of local communities.*

Originality/value – *To date, most studies have focused cross-sectionally on practice characteristics and their association with PCMH adoption. Less understood is how physician practices' PCMH adoption varies as a function of the sociodemographic characteristics of the community in which the practice is located, despite work that acknowledges the importance of social context in decisions about adoption and implementation that can affect the dissemination of innovations.*

Keywords: Patient-centered medical home; community characteristics; longitudinal analysis

INTRODUCTION

The patient-centered medical home (PCMH) has increasingly received attention as a model of care to potentially remedy the cost, quality, and access problems that confront the U.S. health care system (Grumbach & Bodenheimer, 2002; M. B. Rosenthal, 2008). These same problems have generated interest in population health management, defined as "a set of interventions designed to maintain and improve people's health across the full continuum of care – from low-risk, healthy individuals to high-risk individuals with one or more chronic conditions" (Felt-Lisk & Higgins, 2011). For some advocates and policy makers, the PCMH is closely intertwined with population health management (Stange et al., 2010). That is, because many of the core components associated with being a PCMH include activities that would help manage populations of patients (e.g., decision-support systems, patient registry, self-management support), the PCMH is believed to be a promising approach for engaging in population health management where it can have its greatest impact – on the front lines of primary care (T. C. Rosenthal, 2008).

Because of its potential to improve quality and control costs, there have been calls for research to understand the factors that may facilitate or impede its adoption and implementation (Nutting, Miller, & Crabtree, 2009; Rittenhouse & Shortell, 2009; Rittenhouse, Shortell, & Fisher, 2009). Emerging research has begun to identify a number of these factors (Wise, Alexander, Green, Cohen, & Koster, 2011). Much of this research, to date, however, has focused on physician practice-related characteristics and less research has attended to how a physician practice's external environment may influence adoption and implementation decisions. What little research does exist suggests that the external environment acts as an important source of resources that can facilitate or constrain a physician practice's decisions regarding PCMH implementation (Goetz Goldberg & Mick, 2010).

The purpose of this study was to examine physician practices' PCMH capacity, as a function of community characteristics that we argue may reinforce or reduce a physician practice's motivation to implement the PCMH. We assessed these relationships over time for two dimensions of the PCMH (interpersonal and technical), which provided insights into whether physician practices in different types of communities were pursuing different PCMH activities. Likewise, our focus on smaller physician practices, which represent a majority of practices in the United States (Kane, 2009) but are often underrepresented in the research literature, provided insights into the conditions under which these types of practices were thriving or struggling to adopt the PCMH. The longitudinal aspect of the study also provided an opportunity to assess and account for changing trends in PCMH adoption. We believe the study's findings are relevant for PCMH advocates – practitioners and policy makers alike. Policy makers and PCMH program sponsors (e.g., health plans, payers), for example, are likely to have a better understanding of why the distribution of the PCMH may not be even across communities. This knowledge is likely to be important for focusing efforts to further promote the diffusion of the PCMH. A better understanding of whether different types of communities are pursuing different aspects of the PCMH with different levels of success can also help explain why PCMHs in some communities may be more effective than others.

BACKGROUND AND CONCEPTUAL FRAMEWORK

Traditionally, most physician practices have operated as a paternalistic hierarchy where the physician plays the dominant role in decision making (Beisecker & Beisecker, 1993; Brody, 1980). Furthermore, the delivery and financing of health care in the United States has historically reinforced fragmented, episodic care (Bodenheimer, 2008). Therefore, the adoption of the PCMH – defined as a team-based health care delivery model that provides personalized, continuous, and integrated medical care with the goal of improving the health of people, families, and communities (Stange et al., 2010) – is considered a health care delivery system innovation for most physician practices.

Adoption can be defined as the decision "to make full use of an innovation as the best course of action available" (Rogers, 1995, p. 21). The focus of this study, PCMH capacity, can be defined as the ability to offer a service identified as a component part of the PCMH. Thus, PCMH capacity can be considered the outcome of a decision to adopt an innovation, or at least certain components of it in the case of our study. Conceptual models of adoption have identified (at least) three dimensions associated with the adoption process (Rogers, 1995; Wejnert, 2002): (1) characteristics of the innovation (e.g., benefits and costs of an innovation); (2) characteristics of the innovator/adopter (e.g., position in a social network); and (3) environmental context (e.g., geographic settings, political climate). This study examines variations in the adoption of the PCMH as a function of environmental context, controlling for characteristics of the innovator/adopter. Consistent with recent research on the adoption of innovations, we do so using an integrated perspective that combines elements of institutional theory and resource dependence theory to understand how factors external to the organization can influence decisions to adopt (Goetz Goldberg & Mick, 2010; Oliver, 1991; Proenca, Rosko, & Zinn, 2000; Zinn, Weech, & Brannon, 1998).

Institutional Theory

Institutional theory suggests that organizations are subject to different types of isomorphic pressures from external constituents to conform and adopt similar structures and practices (Meyer & Rowan, 1977; Scott, 2001). Coercive isomorphism arises due to pressure from an organization's relationship with entities that an organization depends upon for resources (e.g., accrediting organization, payers, patients). Mimetic isomorphism emerges due to a tendency to imitate successful organizations (e.g., competitors), especially during times of uncertainty. Finally, normative isomorphism arises when organizations follow the standards and expectations established by education and training programs and professional networks. Conformity to these isomorphic pressures helps an organization appear legitimate in the eyes of stakeholders who have control over important resources.

Consistent with arguments that organizations face different types of pressure to adopt similar structures and practices, physician practices today arguably face increasing pressures to pursue PCMH designation. The proliferation of PCMH programs throughout the United States and their linkage to reimbursement and incentives by payers (health insurers and employers) has created significant financial pressure to adopt the PCMH (Patient Centered Primary Care Collaborative, 2009; Takach, 2012). The recent passage of health reform that included provisions related to the PCMH is likely to increase the financial pressures to adopt. The growth in the number of practices seeking PCMH certification (e.g., NCQA) is likely to create competitive pressures to adopt. Physician practices are even likely to feel pressure to adopt from patients as patient-centered care continues to gain momentum and patient awareness of the PCMH grows. Thus, we assume in this study that all physician practices are facing pressure to adopt the PCMH, although the types of pressure and the intensity of this pressure varies across different environments and over time, which influences the PCMH adoption decision and resulting PCMH capacity. Notably, however, given our interest in the sociodemographic characteristics of the environment surrounding the physician practice, we focus on how patients may exert pressure on their physicians to adopt the PCMH.

Resource Dependence Theory

In contrast to institutional theory, which assumes an organization's adoption decision is constrained by a desire to conform to external pressures and appear legitimate, resource dependence theorists argue that organizational decision makers are rational and managers undertake certain courses of action to acquire critical resources and reduce dependence on other organizations in their external environment (Aldrich & Pfeffer, 1976; Pfeffer & Salancik, 1978). Resource dependence theorists often distinguish between three different dimensions of the external environment (Dess & Beard, 1984).

Munificence refers to the abundance and availability of resources in the environment. Dynamism refers to the rate of change in the environment. Complexity reflects the range of elements that need to be taken into consideration by an organization (e.g., other providers, patient groups, insurance companies).

According to research using resource dependence theory, organizations that operate in more munificent environments are more likely to adopt innovations (e.g., electronic health records; Balotsky, 2005). In contrast, more dynamic and complex environments present more uncertainty for organizations with respect to whether their investment in an innovation will yield the expected benefits and whether an innovation can be adopted and implemented in a consistent, "one size fits all" manner (Rogers, 1995; Walker, 2007). Thus, more complex environments may require organizations to modify an innovation or adopt multiple versions of it to fit the differentiated needs of its diverse environment. Such approaches are likely more costly to adopt and more difficult to implement as they require novel integration strategies that cannot easily be imitated.

Based on these combined perspectives, we generally submit that practices located in environments that exert greater institutional pressure and with more abundant resources will be associated with higher levels of PCMH capacity, while practices located in environments reflective of greater complexity will be associated with lower levels of PCMH capacity. In the following sections, we expand on these ideas by applying them to the structural characteristics of the external environment, namely the sociodemographic characteristics (i.e., socioeconomic status, race/ethnicity, and age) in the community surrounding the physician practice. We combine our discussion of socioeconomic status and race/ethnicity due to similar mechanisms by which these characteristics may influence PCMH capacity as well as research showing that racial and ethnic minorities are disproportionately represented in lower socioeconomic ranks (Institute of Medicine, 2003; Williams, 1999; Williams & Collins, 1995).

Socioeconomic Status (SES) and Race/Ethnicity

Minorities and lower SES individuals have historically faced systemic discrimination (both implicitly and explicitly) in the U.S. health care system (Institute of Medicine, 2003). As a result, lower SES individuals and racial/ethnic minorities are often less trusting of institutions such as the health care system, including physicians (Boulware, Cooper, Ratner,

LaVeist, & Powe, 2003; Doescher, Saver, Franks, & Fiscella, 2000). Lower trust is associated with less civic participation and health care advocacy; thus, lower SES individuals and racial/ethnic minorities are less likely to have their views represented by political and organizational leaders (Bartels, 2003; Brady, Verba, & Schlozman, 1995; Uslaner & Brown, 2005).

Research has also shown that individuals of lower SES and racial/ethnic minorities often do not have access to the same number and same quality of informational resources as individuals of higher SES (Brodie et al., 2000; Institute of Medicine, 2003). One potential consequence of this informational gap is that individuals of lower SES and racial/ethnic minorities may be less likely to possess knowledge of innovations such as the PCMH, or are more likely to learn of it later. Furthermore, individuals of lower SES and minorities are more likely to take a more passive role when it comes to their interactions with health care professionals (Kaplan, Gandek, Greenfield, Rogers, & Ware, 1995; Levinson, Kao, Kuby, & Thisted, 2005), and therefore may be less likely to exert coercive pressure on their physicians. Together, this research suggests that physician practices may face fewer pressures to adopt the PCMH when located in environments with a lower level of SES and a higher percentage of minorities.

From a resource perspective, pressures and opportunities to adopt the PCMH in geographic areas with lower SES and higher numbers of racial/ethnic minorities are mixed. On one hand, to the extent these communities suffer from lower access and worse health outcomes, they have the most need and have the most to gain from new care delivery models that can ameliorate these problems (Rogers, 1995). On the other hand, areas of lower SES often have fewer resources to support and justify the adoption and implementation of innovations (Damanpour, 1991; Nohria & Gulati, 1996) such as the PCMH. Despite these mixed motivations, most research has found that greater availability of resources is associated with greater innovation adoption and a lack of resources inhibits it (Damanpour, 1991; Nohria & Gulati, 1996).

Hypothesis 1. PCMH capacity will be lower among practices in geographic areas with lower socioeconomic status.

Hypothesis 2. PCMH capacity will be lower among practices in geographic areas with a greater percentage of minorities.

As noted earlier, environmental complexity can have a dampening effect on the adoption of innovations. Higher numbers of low SES individuals typically reflect greater income inequality in a geographic area, which presents a more complex environment for physician practices due to more diverse needs of residents in the area (e.g., health services, social services). Higher numbers of low SES individuals also reflect a greater range of education and employment situations, and thus may require different approaches to meet the differentiated needs of the community. Similarly, a wider range of racial/ethnic minorities in a community presents greater complexity because of more differentiated health care needs and more varied expectations about how health care should be delivered due to the different social and cultural backgrounds. Therefore, it is hypothesized that:

> **Hypothesis 3.** PCMH capacity will be lower among practices in geographic areas with more diverse socioeconomic status.

> **Hypothesis 4.** PCMH capacity will be lower in geographic areas with greater racial/ethnic heterogeneity.

Age

Similar to SES and the racial/ethnic composition of the local area, the age composition of the environment surrounding a physician practice is likely to influence the knowledge and participation levels of community residents, which we submit will generate different levels of coercive pressure on physician practices to adopt the PCMH. However, research related to age is mixed with respect to its predicted effect on knowledge and participation (Rogers, 1995). On one hand, older individuals have more diverse experiences, which can enhance the knowledge base that these individuals draw upon when forming expectations of their care providers (Glenn & Grimes, 1968). Likewise, because they are more likely to have acquired more information, older adults may have developed a more sophisticated framework for processing new information (Cho & McLeod, 2007). On the other hand, research on patient engagement and participation suggests that older adults do not necessarily act upon this knowledge. For example, research indicates that preferences for an active role in health care decision making increases up to age 45 and then declines (Levinson et al., 2005), while other research has found that older adults had less participatory visits with their physicians (Kaplan et al., 1995; Stiggelbout & Kiebert, 1997). Thus, it is unclear what level of coercive pressure might be expected from an older population. Goetz Goldberg and Mick (2010) argue, however, that higher percentages of Medicare beneficiaries (i.e., an older population) result in coercive pressure on physician practices to adopt innovations that improve practice efficiency and effectiveness due to rules and regulations imposed by payers such as Medicare that predominantly pays for physician services for the elderly.

From a resource perspective, an older population likely represents a significant source of resources to adopt the PCMH. As noted above, older individuals (over 65) are covered by Medicare, which represents a relatively reliable source of reimbursement for physician practices. Furthermore, older adults typically have more chronic conditions, on average, than younger adults (Ward & Schiller, 2013) and have consistent demand for physician services. The PCMH's origins and many of its current capabilities focus on the management of patients with complex health needs such as those with chronic conditions. Therefore, one might expect physician practices in areas with an older population to adopt innovations to better suit the needs of this population.

Hypothesis 5. PCMH capacity will be higher among practices in geographic areas with a greater percentage of older residents.

Similar to environments with greater SES and racial/ethnic heterogeneity, we expect environments with more age diversity to present more complex environments for physician practices due to their differentiated needs and more varied expectations about how health care should be delivered. Therefore, it is hypothesized that:

Hypothesis 6. PCMH capacity will be lower in geographic areas with greater age heterogeneity.

METHODS

Study Setting

The study focused on primary care and specialty care physician practices that were members of a consortium of physician organizations participating in the Blue Cross Blue Shield of Michigan's (BCBSM) *Physician Group Incentive Program* (PGIP). PGIP is a unique statewide initiative that works directly with physician organizations (e.g., independent physician associations, physician hospital organizations, medical groups) to help constituent practices (e.g., process redesign consulting, performance reporting) implement structural and processual features of the PCMH (Share & Mason,

2012). The consortium consisted of 48 physician organizations throughout the state of Michigan, representing 831 physician practices and 1,673 physicians. Our study, however, focused on practices continuously enrolled in the program from 2008 through 2012; thus, 523 practices were included in the analysis. By PGIP design, these practices included the following specialties: family practice, general medicine, internal medicine, pediatrics, allergy/immunology, cardiology, endocrinology, and pulmonology. Given the focus on these specialties, primary care practices were overrepresented in our sample, with over 70% of the sample practices being primary care compared to 34% for the rest of Michigan.

The BCBSM PCMH program is organized into different dimensions, or domains, that were initially identified by BCBSM based on the Patient-Centered Primary Care Collaborative's Joint Principles (PCPCC). After identifying these domains, subject matter expert teams (i.e., physicians and nurses) were assembled for each domain to identify the key components of each domain as well as discrete, measurable steps (i.e., capabilities) that would indicate incremental progress in that domain. Interpretive guidelines were also developed to assist practices in understanding these domains and their respective capabilities. A recent review of different PCMH programs by the Urban Institute suggests that the 12 domains included in the BCBSM PGIP put more emphasis on care coordination, quality measurement, patient engagement and self-management, and population management than other large PCMH programs (e.g., NCQA, TransforMED) and less emphasis on formal policies and comprehensiveness of care.

Data Collection

Data were collected from physician practices with an electronic survey that asked whether the practice was capable of engaging in specific activities or capabilities associated with the PCMH (e.g., after-hours accessibility, use of registry with evidence-based guidelines; Table 1). Because eligibility for incentive dollars was tied to responses to this survey, all physician practices completed surveys. Respondents indicated whether a practice had a capability by responding "In Place" or "Not in Place." As of December 2012, surveys had been administered to physician practices at 10 points in time: October 2008, February 2009, May 2009, December 2009, June 2010, December 2010, July 2011, December 2011, July 2012, and December 2012. The first two surveys included activities associated with six domains of the PCMH: (1) patient-provider partnership; (2) patient registry;

Table 1. PCMH Domain Descriptions.

Domain	Description/Purpose	Number of Capabilities
Extended access	Ensure that all patients have comprehensive and timely access to health care services that are patient centered, culturally sensitive, and delivered in the least intensive and most appropriate setting based on the patient's needs.	9
Individual care management	Ensure that patients with chronic conditions receive organized, planned care from a team of multi-disciplinary providers.	15
Patient-provider partnership	Expand physician and patient awareness of, and commitment to, the patient-centered medical home model and strengthen the bond between patients and their care-giving team.	8
Patient registry	Establish a comprehensive patient registry that can be used to optimally manage a population of patients, improve health status, and ultimately lower health care costs.	18
Performance reporting	Implement reporting technology that will allow providers to generate point of care reports, population-level reports, and trend analyses to identify opportunities for improving care delivered to patients.	12
Test result tracking and follow-up	Implement a standardized, reliable system to ensure that patients receive needed tests, results are communicated in a timely manner, follow-up appropriate to the patient case is conducted, and each step in the test tracking process is properly documented.	9
Preventive services[a]	Establish systematic procedures in the practice unit to actively counsel patients on primary and secondary preventive care.	8
Linkage to community services[a]	Enable a physician practice to have knowledge of, and collaborative relationships with key community resources, and assist patients in receiving needed community services through a systematic process for referrals and follow-up.	8
Self-management support[a]	Educate all members of the practice unit's clinical team about self-management support concepts and techniques, including health literacy and motivational interviewing.	8
Patient web portal[a]	Support optimal management of patients with chronic conditions by using a patient web portal to allow for electronic communication between patients and physicians, and provide greater access to medical information and technical tools.	12

Table 1. (*Continued*)

Domain	Description/Purpose	Number of Capabilities
Coordination of care[a]	Improve coordination of patient care across the health system through a process of active collaboration and communication between the patient, providers, and care-givers.	9
Specialist referral process[a]	Create a well-coordinated, seamless process of referring patients from primary care to specialty care.	9
Total		125

[a]Domains were added in 2009.

(3) performance reporting; (4) individual care management; (5) extended access; and (6) test tracking and follow-up. There were 71 capabilities included across these six domains. Six additional domains were added between February and May 2009: (1) preventive services; (2) linkage to community services; (3) self-management support; (4) patient web portal; (5) coordination of care; and (6) specialist referral process. Fifty-four additional capabilities were added with these six domains, for a total of 125 PCMH capabilities.

Measures

PCMH Capacity

PCMH capacity was assessed with two variables, interpersonal capacity and technical capacity. Interpersonal capacity was constructed to reflect process- or service-oriented aspects of the PCMH. Interpersonal capacity was measured as the sum of capabilities (1 = "In Place" and 0 = "Not in Place") for the following eight domains consistent with those that Ferrante, Balasubramanian, Hudson, and Crabtree (2010) identified as "high touch": (1) coordination of care; (2) individual care management; (3) linkage to community services; (4) patient-provider partnership; (5) preventive services; (6) self-management support; (7) specialist referral process; and (8) test result tracking and follow-up. Because the number of possible capabilities varied over time, we chose to analyze this variable as the percentage of possible capabilities in place (i.e., number of capabilities in place divided by the number of capabilities possible, multiplied by 100).

Technical capacity, in contrast, reflected more structural aspects of the PCMH. It was measured as the sum of capabilities (1 = "In Place" and 0 = "Not in Place") for the following four domains consistent with those that Ferrante et al. (2010) identified as "high tech": (1) extended access; (2) patient registry; (3) performance reporting; and (4) patient web portal.

Sociodemographic Characteristics

In order to assess the extent to which the external environment surrounding the practice was associated with PCMH capacity, we included six variables related to three sociodemographic characteristics: (1) SES; (2) race and ethnicity; and (3) age. Each sociodemographic category included two variables – one variable was included to assess the average level or intensity of a characteristic and a second variable was included to capture the heterogeneity related to that same characteristic (i.e., designed to capture complexity). *Average county-level SES* was a composite measure of SES constructed by standardizing four variables ((1) percentage of county residents below federal poverty level; (2) percentage of county residents with less than a high school education; (3) percentage of county residents that were unemployed; and (4) percentage of county residents that were uninsured) and summing across these variables. We opted for this composite measure over independent covariates to parsimoniously yet comprehensively assess the multiple dimensions of SES. *SES heterogeneity* was calculated as the average difference between each of the four SES variables (e.g., the absolute value of the percentage of residents below federal poverty subtracted from the percentage of residents that were unemployed). Thus, this variable indicated how similar or different county residents were with respect to the four dimensions of SES that we included in the study, with higher values reflecting a more heterogeneous population with respect to SES. *Percent minority* was calculated as the number of racial and ethnic minorities (i.e., Blacks, Hispanics, Asians, and Others) in a county divided by the total number of county residents, multiplied by 100. *Racial and ethnic heterogeneity* was measured with Blau's index of heterogeneity (Blau, 1977) using five county-level racial and ethnic groups: (1) proportion of county residents that were White; (2) proportion of county residents that were Black; (3) proportion of county residents that were Hispanic; (4) proportion of county residents that were Asian; and (5) proportion of county residents that were some other race or ethnicity. Consistent with Blau (1977) and other research (Bantel & Jackson, 1989; Harrison, Price, & Bell, 1998), the index was constructed as $1 - \Sigma pi^2$, where p was the proportion of residents in a county from the ith racial and ethnic group. *Percent over 65* was calculated as the number of county residents over the age of 65 divided by the total number of county residents, multiplied by 100. *Age heterogeneity* was also measured with Blau's index of heterogeneity using four county-level age groups: (1) proportion of county residents between the ages of 0 and 14; (2) the proportion of county residents between the ages of 15 and 44; (3) the proportion of county residents between the ages of 45 and 64; and (4) the proportion of county residents over the age of 65.

Control Variables

We also controlled for a number of practice characteristics that previous research has identified as playing an important role in PCMH adoption specifically and adoption decisions more generally, including: (1) type of physician organization; (2) number of physicians in a practice; (3) practice specialty; and (4) presence of an electronic medical record (EMR) at baseline. Physician practices in the consortium participated in PGIP through five different types of larger organizational entities: (1) community health centers; (2) physician hospital organizations; (3) independent physician associations; (4) medical groups; and (5) hospital-employed physicians. Physician practices were grouped into one of four size categories: (1) solo practitioner; (2) two to three physicians; (3) four to seven physicians; and (4) eight or more physicians. Practice specialty was based on the types of specialties represented by physicians in the practice, with practices being grouped into four types: (1) family practice (including general medicine); (2) internal medicine; (3) pediatrics; and (4) specialist (including allergy, cardiology, endocrinology, and pulmonology). EMR at baseline was a dichotomous indicator of whether the practice had an EMR in the initial assessment period (1 = "Yes" and 0 = "No"). We also controlled for two additional geographic area attributes associated with adoption decisions. Provider supply/concentration was captured with three dummy variables that indicated whether a practice was: (1) located in a county designated as a Health Professional Shortage Area (HPSA); (2) located in a county that was partially designated as a HPSA; and (3) located in a county not designated as a HPSA (referent). Likewise, population density was captured with three dummy variables corresponding with three types of counties: (1) urban; (2) suburban; or (3) rural (referent).

Time

Because the time between measurement periods varied, we chose to use a more flexible measure of time based on month increments, with October

2008 serving as the baseline month (Singer & Willett, 2003). Thus, the time variable can be interpreted as the increase or decrease in PCMH capacity associated with each additional month.

Analytic Strategy

The unit of analysis was the physician practice. Univariate statistics were used to describe variations in PCMH capacity across practices and over time. Multivariate relationships between PCMH capacity and community characteristics were assessed using linear growth models. Linear growth curve models are a type of hierarchical linear model, where each practice's change in PCMH capacity can be represented by a growth trajectory (i.e., level-1) and these growth parameters become the outcome variables in a level-2 model where they may vary as a function of practice characteristics (Raudenbush & Bryk, 2002). This analytic approach allowed us to account for research suggesting the physician practices follow different developmental pathways when pursuing the PCMH (Nutting et al., 2010).

Growth models also allowed us to partition the overall variation in PCMH capacity into its component parts (i.e., variation between practices vs. variation within practices). To do so, we first estimated an unconditional means model (i.e., no covariates) to estimate how much variability in PCMH capacity existed across practices (via the intraclass correlation coefficient, or ICC), followed by an unconditional growth model (i.e., added the time covariate) to examine changes in PCMH capacity over time. In the third step, we entered the practice characteristics into the unconditional growth model and compared the covariance parameter estimates from each of these models to the unconditional growth model to assess how much variation in PCMH capacity was explained by these characteristics. Finally, in the fourth step, we entered the community characteristics into the model that included the practice characteristics and compared the covariance parameters from this model with those from the model with just the practice characteristics to assess how much additional variation was explained by the community characteristics. We used a pseudo-R^2 that correlated the predicted values from the full model with the observed values to assess how much of the total variation was explained by the models. SAS PROC MIXED was used for all analyses (Littell, Milliken, Stroup, & Wolfinger, 1996; SAS Institute Inc., 2004; Singer, 1998).

RESULTS

Univariate Results

Physician practices participating through independent physician associations were most prevalent in our sample (53.7%), followed by physician hospital organizations (23.3%), community health centers (8.8%), medical groups (8.6%), and hospital employed (5.4%; Table 2). Family practice was the most common specialty in our sample (51.1%), followed by internal medicine (28.5%), pediatrics (9.6%), and specialist (4.9%) practices. Solo practitioner physician practices were most common in our sample (67.1%), followed by practices with two or three physicians (19.7%), practices with four to seven physicians (9.4%), and practices with eight or more physicians (3.8%). About one third of the practices (35.3%) had an EMR at baseline. Physician practices located in a county that was partially designated as a HPSA were most common in our sample (71.3%), followed by those located in a county wholly designated as a HPSA (26.6%), and physician practices located in a county not designated as a HPSA (2.1%). Likewise, physician practices located in an urban county accounted for 52.7% of our sample, followed by rural (23.9%) and suburban (23.4%).

The technical dimension exhibited the lowest level of capacity across the physician practices in the initial time period (Table 3). On average, physician practices had adopted only 1.6% of the technical capabilities possible compared to 3.9% of the interpersonal capabilities. By the final period, physician practices had adopted 38.5% of the total interpersonal capabilities and12.5% of the technical capabilities.

Interpersonal Capacity

Interpersonal capacity increased by 1.1% per month, on average, over the 51-month period included in the study (Table 4). Practices located in counties with more heterogeneous SES were associated with lower levels of interpersonal capacity ($b = -0.97$, $p < 0.001$). Similarly, practices located in counties in with higher levels of age heterogeneity were associated with lower interpersonal capacity, on average ($b = -131.25$, $p < 0.001$). In contrast, practices in counties with a higher percentage of residents over the age of 65 were associated with higher levels of interpersonal capacity ($b = 1.46$, $p < 0.001$).

Table 2. Baseline Physician Practice and Community Characteristics ($N = 523$).

Type of physician organization	
Hospital-based (*N*/%)	29/5.54%
Community health center (*N*/%)	46/8.80%
Physician hospital organization (*N*/%)	122/23.33%
Independent physician association (*N*/%)	281/53.73%
Medical group (*N*/%)	45/8.60%
Practice specialty	
Family practice (*N*/%)	267/51.05%
Internal medicine (*N*/%)	149/28.49%
Pediatrics (*N*/%)	50/9.56%
Specialist (*N*/%)	57/10.90%
Practice size	
Solo practice (*N*/%)	351/67.11%
2–3 practitioners (*N*/%)	103/19.69%
4–7 practitioners (*N*/%)	49/9.37%
8 or more practitioners (*N*/%)	20/3.82%
EMR use at baseline (*N*/%)	171/35.26%
HPSA	
Whole HPSA (*N*/%)	139/26.6%
Part HPSA (*N*/%)	372/71.3%
Not an HPSA (*N*/%)	11/2.1%
Urban/rural	
Urban (*N*/%)	275/52.68%
Suburban (*N*/%)	122/23.37%
Rural (*N*/%)	125/23.95%
Community characteristics	
SES composite (*M*/SD)	−1.68/2.10
SES heterogeneity index (*M*/SD)	4.73/3.20
Percent minority (*M*/SD)	13.06/11.39
Race diversity index (*M*/SD)	0.46/0.26
Percent older than 65 (*M*/SD)	7.64/1.99
Age heterogeneity index (*M*/SD)	0.71/0.03

Table 3. PCMH Capacity by Time.

Capacity	Percent of Capabilities in Place								
	Time 1	Time 2	Time 3	Time 4	Time 5	Time 6	Time 7	Time 8	Time 9
Technical	1.62	3.27	3.71	6.78	9.89	11.77	12.38	11.64	12.47
Interpersonal	3.89	5.59	9.61	17.40	30.37	36.75	38.58	37.46	38.54

Technical Capacity

Technical capacity increased by 0.3% per month, on average, over the 51-month period included in the study (Table 4). Among the sociodemographic characteristics, county-level SES, SES heterogeneity index, percent over 65 years old, and age heterogeneity were significantly associated with technical capacity. Practices located in counties with a one-unit lower SES were associated with a 0.4% higher level of technical capacity, on average

Table 4. Linear Growth Curve Results ($N = 523$).

	Interpersonal	Technical
	b (SE)	*b* (SE)
Time	1.06 (0.03)***	0.33 (0.02)***
Sociodemographic characteristics		
SES composite	0.40 (0.22)	0.40 (0.09)***
SES heterogeneity index	−0.97 (0.19)***	−0.41 (0.08)***
Percent minority	−0.04 (0.28)	−0.08 (0.16)
Race heterogeneity index	9.93 (22.80)	8.11 (13.04)
Percent over 65	1.46 (0.48)***	1.04 (0.28)***
Age heterogeneity index	−131.25 (40.19)***	−77.81 (22.54)***
Control variables		
Hospital employed	Referent	Referent
Community health center	4.90 (2.89)	6.54 (1.70)***
Physician hospital organization	2.50 (2.73)	3.23 (1.61)*
Independent physician organization	−1.60 (2.55)	0.88 (1.50)
Medical group	−1.41 (3.13)	1.36 (1.84)
2–3 practitioners	−0.72 (1.28)	−1.09 (0.75)
4–7 practitioners	3.85 (1.68)*	1.32 (0.99)
8 or more practitioners	2.68 (2.42)	−1.17 (1.42)
Solo practitioner	Referent	Referent
EMR use baseline	2.60 (1.08)*	0.91 (0.64)
Specialists	Referent	
Pediatrics	4.29 (2.21)*	−1.59 (1.30)
Family practice	3.60 (1.75)*	−1.53 (1.03)
Internal medicine	1.55 (1.85)	−1.07 (1.09)
Not an HPSA	Referent	Referent
Whole HPSA	−6.71 (3.98)	−9.42 (2.31)***
Part HPSA	−4.31 (3.52)	−8.12 (2.05)***
Rural	Referent	Referent
Suburban	5.80 (2.00)***	1.63 (1.17)
Urban	8.19 (2.22)***	2.71 (1.30)*

*$p < 0.05$; **$p < 0.01$; ***$p < 0.001$.

($b = 0.40$, $p < 0.001$). Practices in counties with a more heterogeneous SES population were associated with lower levels of technical capacity ($b = -0.41$, $p < 0.001$). Practices located in counties with a higher percentage of residents over the age of 65 were associated with higher levels of technical capacity, on average ($b = 1.04$, $p < 0.001$), while practices in counties in with higher levels of age heterogeneity were associated with lower technical capacity ($b = -77.81$, $p < 0.001$).

Control Variables

There were also a number of significant relationships between PCMH capacity and the control variables included in the analysis as well. In general, community health centers and physician hospital organizations reported higher levels of technical capacity compared to hospital-based physician practices. Similarly, relative to solo practitioners, practices consisting of four to seven physicians were associated with higher interpersonal capacity. Practices with an EMR at baseline were associated with higher levels of interpersonal capacity, but not technical capacity. Pediatric and family practice practices reported higher levels of interpersonal capacity relative to specialists. Relative to physician practices located in a county not designated as a HPSA, practices located in counties that were designated as an HPSA (partially or wholly) were associated with lower levels of technical capacity. Finally, physician practices located in urban or suburban counties, on average, were associated with higher levels of interpersonal capacity, relative to practices in rural counties. Similarly, physician practices in urban counties were associated with higher levels of technical capacity compared to practices in rural counties.

Variance in PCMH Capacity

Overall, time and the practice and community characteristics considered in this study accounted for a relatively wide range of the total variation in PCMH capacity, explaining 16.8% of the total variation in technical capacity, 39.3% of the interpersonal capacity. Notably, however, the sociodemographic characteristics that were of primary theoretical interest only accounted for an additional 1.1% and 1.6% of the total variation for interpersonal and technical capacity, respectively, beyond the variation explained by practice characteristics and time. Finally, our analysis of the intraclass correlation coefficients indicated that more of the variation in technical capacity was between physician practices rather than within practices over time. Specifically, our analysis indicated that 63.1% of the variation in technical capacity was due to variations between physician practices. In contrast, only 42.4% of the total variation in interpersonal capacity was due to variations between practices, indicating that practices did not differ as much with respect to their interpersonal capabilities, as compared to technical capabilities.

DISCUSSION

The purpose of this study was to examine PCMH capacity as a function of community-level sociodemographic characteristics. The analysis yielded a number of findings that are likely to be of interest to policy makers, practitioners, and others who are interested in the PCMH as a means of engaging in population health in primary care physician practices and improving health care quality and costs. First, our finding that lower SES of the surrounding geographic area was associated with higher technical capacity was not what was expected based on our theoretical framework. Resource dependence theory, in particular, suggests that fewer resources in the community would be associated with lower levels of PCMH adoption. Other research, however, has found that practices that serve disproportionate shares of patients residing in economically disadvantaged neighborhoods were actually more likely to have structural capabilities associated with the PCMH, such as an electronic health record and on-site language interpreters (Friedberg, Coltin, Safran, Dresser, & Schneider, 2010). Consistent with explanations provided by these researchers, one potential explanation for our finding is that the physician practices that were included in our study (i.e., participants in an incentive program sponsored by a large commercial insurer) are not the types of practices that are most likely to be influenced by the SES of surrounding geographical areas. Even so, the findings are likely to be encouraging to PCMH advocates hoping to achieve more widespread adoption because they suggest that practices in more socioeconomic disadvantaged areas are not eschewing the PCMH, at least not for technical components and not more so than practices in more socioeconomically advantaged areas. Likewise, advocates of the PCMH who believe that it can help ameliorate disparities in care (Anderson & Olayiwola, 2012) may find these findings encouraging as they indicate that practices located in the areas where the PCMH may have some of its most important impact are in fact adopting these capabilities.

Our analysis also showed that geographic areas with a more diverse socioeconomic population had lower PCMH capacity, for both interpersonal and technical dimensions of the PCMH, which is consistent with other research suggesting that more complex environments inhibit the adoption of innovations (Pfeffer & Salancik, 1978; Walker, 2007). One explanation, as suggested earlier, is that a more diverse socioeconomic population requires a greater variety of approaches to meet the differentiated needs of the community and that physician practices that recognize these challenges may question the ability of the PCMH to satisfy all these needs, at least without significant modifications. Future research is needed, however, to assess whether this is, in fact the case, or whether more diverse socioeconomic conditions exert this suppressive effect in other ways.

Our analysis did not find any significant relationships between racial and ethnic characteristics of surrounding geographic areas and PCMH capacity, for either the overall percentage of minorities or for the racial/ethnic diversity of the area. The finding related to overall percentage of minorities is also consistent with other research that has found that a physician practice's patient mix is not significantly associated with use of PCMH processes (Friedberg et al., 2010; Rittenhouse et al., 2011). Again, one explanation for these findings is that the physician practices that are included in our study are not the types of practices that are most likely to be influenced by the racial and ethnic composition of the surrounding geographical areas. Another possibility is that the knowledge gap about the PCMH and differences in the subsequent demands for adoption of the PCMH is not as pronounced as we hypothesized. Future research that assesses the level of awareness and knowledge about the PCMH among patients would be helpful in determining which of these explanations is more accurate. Regardless, and similar to the SES of the surrounding population, PCMH advocates trying to achieve more widespread adoption may find these findings encouraging as they indicate that the level of PCMH adoption is not suppressed in areas that may stand to benefit disproportionately from this innovation.

Among the sociodemographic characteristics considered in the study, age exhibited the most consistent relationships. Specifically, our analysis indicated that practices located in geographic areas with an older population and a less diverse population with respect to age had adopted a higher number of PCMH capabilities. Given that older adults are more likely to be diagnosed with a chronic disease and thus have greater health care needs, these findings are likely to be encouraging to those who believe that the PCMH is well suited to meet these needs (Rich, Lipson, Libersky, Peikes, & Parchman, 2012).

Although our primary interest was in the sociodemographic characteristics of the geographic area surrounding a physician practice, our analysis did find a number of control variables significantly associated with PCMH capacity. Our analysis showed that, relative to physician practices located in rural areas, practices located in suburban and urban areas were associated with higher levels of both interpersonal and technical capacity. Likewise, physician practices located in counties designated as HPSAs (partial or full) were associated with lower levels of technical capacity. One explanation for these findings can also be found in institutional theory. Specifically, conformity to the institutional environment is dependent on the degree of interconnectedness between organizations (Oliver, 1991). Greater interconnectedness promotes sharing of information, values, and practices between organizations, and in doing so, fosters greater normative and mimetic pressure to adopt innovations such as the PCMH (Oliver, 1991; Rogers, 1995). Thus, pressures to adopt the PCMH are expected to be lower in geographic areas where there fewer opportunities to establish relationships with other providers (i.e., lower provider supply, less densely populated). Furthermore, from a resource dependence perspective, geographic areas with fewer providers and residents are likely to have less competition (Feldman & Sloan, 1988) and less competition is likely to reduce a physician practice's need to differentiate itself from competitors (Goetz Goldberg & Mick, 2010). More research is needed, however, to assess why the relationship between PCMH capacity and a practice's location in a HPSA was limited to technical capabilities.

Given the longitudinal design of the study, another interesting finding pertains to the relationship between time and PCMH capacity. Our analysis found that PCMH capacity increased over time, especially for interpersonal capabilities. The rate of change for interpersonal capacity was over three times the rate of change for technical capabilities. One explanation for this difference is that interpersonal capacity arguably captures activities that physicians have traditionally engaged in (e.g., referrals, care coordination), while technical capacity captures activities that are more novel to physician practices, and therefore more disruptive. Consistent with this idea, Nutting et al. (2009) found that practices pursuing the PCMH found the implementation of new technology more difficult than imagined, even for those who already had an EMR. Likewise, it is also possible that the resources required to implement these different capabilities differ across the two dimensions. For example, time and effort is required for many of the interpersonal capabilities, but time, effort, *and* financial capital are required for technical capabilities. Regardless, future research that continues to explore the reasons for these differential rates of growth would be helpful for fostering greater levels of adoption. Furthermore, to the extent that these different capabilities are associated with different health behaviors and outcomes, a better understanding of why these capabilities grow at different rates may help prevent unbalanced adoption and the varying outcomes that may emerge as a consequence.

Finally, the sociodemographic characteristics included in our study accounted for a relatively small amount of variation in PCMH capacity, above and beyond time and practice characteristics. One explanation for this finding is that sociodemographic characteristics are simply not the primary driving force behind PCMH adoption. Another possibility is that other types of environmental characteristics are more important drivers of adoption, such as delivery system characteristics (e.g., managed care penetration, competition). While our study controlled for a number of characteristics that are arguably related to the delivery system (e.g., HPSA), there are undoubtedly others that may be important to consider in future research. For example, Rittenhouse et al. (2011) found that higher levels of external incentives were associated with greater use of medical home processes.

It is also interesting that our covariance analysis found higher levels of variation between practices with respect to technical capabilities as compared to interpersonal capabilities. One explanation, as suggested earlier, is that interpersonal capabilities are skills and tasks that practices have historically provided for patients. Thus, more physician practices have accumulated experience with these capabilities over time, leading to less variation between practices. In contrast, technological capabilities may be more disruptive and require more and different types of resources to adopt, thus practices have been more reluctant to adopt these types of capabilities. Regardless, future research on why variations between practices differ for interpersonal and technical capabilities would enhance our understanding of differential adoption patterns.

There are a number of limitations that should be considered when interpreting these findings. First, the physician practices included in the study were located in a single state, and therefore may not be representative of all physician practices. Similarly, the PCMH program examined in this study was designed specifically as part of a larger pay-for-performance program, thus, the incentives and challenges to adoption and implementation may differ from other types of PCMH programs. Our analysis also focused on practices continuously enrolled in the program, thus, it does not reflect the adoption patterns of practices that quit the program or joined the program in later years. Finally, the study focused on smaller sized physician practices, with most physician practices being solo practitioners or practices with two or three physicians, and thus may not be generalizable to larger physician practices. Nevertheless, given the paucity of research on smaller physician practices, we believe our findings provide valuable insights into how these practices may be influenced by their external environment. It is also notable that the level of adoption reported in our study is consistent with estimates provided by other research analyzing PCMH processes in smaller sized physician practices (Rittenhouse et al., 2011).

CONCLUSION

The PCMH has received a growing amount of attention in recent years as a means of improving the quality of care received by patients. As a result, PCMH programs have proliferated and practitioners have been actively pursuing the adoption and implementation of these programs. Our research indicates, however, that PCMH capabilities may not be evenly distributed across communities and raise questions about whether such distributional differences influence the PCMH's ability to improve population health, especially the health of vulnerable populations. Likewise, our research suggests that only certain environmental factors are associated with PCMH adoption and amongst those that are, they can exhibit facilitative, inhibitive, and nonsignificant effects on PCMH adoption depending upon the dimension of PCMH capacity one is considering. Such nuances highlight the challenges faced by practitioners and policy makers who advocate the continued expansion of the PCMH.

ACKNOWLEDGMENTS

This research was supported by a grant from the Agency for Healthcare Research and Quality and the University of Alabama at Birmingham's Center for Outcomes and Effectiveness Research and Education.

REFERENCES

Aldrich, H. E., & Pfeffer, J. (1976). Environments of organizations. *Annual Review of Sociology*, *2*, 79–105.

Anderson, D. R., & Olayiwola, J. N. (2012). Community health centers and the patient-centered medical home: Challenges and opportunities to reduce health care disparities in America. *Journal of Health Care for the Poor and Underserved*, *23*(3), 949–957.

Balotsky, E. R. (2005). Is it resources, habit or both: Interpreting twenty years of hospital strategic response to prospective payment. *Health Care Management Review*, *30*(4), 337–346.

Bantel, K. A., & Jackson, S. E. (1989). Top management and innovations in banking: Does the composition of the top team make a difference? *Strategic Management Journal*, *10*(S1), 107–124.

Bartels, L. M. (2003). Democracy with attitudes. In *Electoral democracy* (pp. 48–82). Ann Arbor, MI: University of Michigan.

Beisecker, A. E., & Beisecker, T. D. (1993). Using metaphors to characterize doctor-patient relationships: Paternalism versus consumerism. *Health Communication*, *5*(1), 41–58.

Blau, P. M. (1977). *Inequality and heterogeneity: A primitive theory of social structure*. New York, NY: Free Press.

Bodenheimer, T. (2008). Coordinating care – A perilous journey through the health care system. *New England Journal of Medicine*, *358*(10), 1064.

Boulware, L. E., Cooper, L. A., Ratner, L. E., LaVeist, T. A., & Powe, N. R. (2003). Race and trust in the health care system. *Public Health Reports*, *118*(4), 358.

Brady, H. E., Verba, S., & Schlozman, K. L. (1995). Beyond SES: A resource model of political participation. *American Political Science Review*, *89*(2), 271–294.

Brodie, M. A., Flournoy, R. E., Altman, D., Blendon, R. J., Benson, J. M., & Rosenbaum, M. D. (2000). Health information, the internet, and the digital divide. *Health Affairs*, *19*(6), 255–265.

Brody, D. (1980). The patient's role in clinical decision-making. *Annals of Internal Medicine*, *93*(5), 718–722.

Cho, J., & McLeod, D. M. (2007). Structural antecedents to knowledge and participation: Extending the knowledge gap concept to participation. *Journal of Communication*, *57*(2), 205–228.

Damanpour, F. (1991). Organizational innovation: A meta-analysis of effects of determinants and moderators. *Academy of Management Journal*, *34*(3), 555–590.

Dess, G. G., & Beard, D. W. (1984). Dimensions of organizational task environments. *Administrative Science Quarterly*, *29*(1), 52–73.

Doescher, M. P., Saver, B. G., Franks, P., & Fiscella, K. (2000). Racial and ethnic disparities in perceptions of physician style and trust. *Archives of Family Medicine*, *9*, 1156–1163.

Feldman, R., & Sloan, F. (1988). Competition among physicians, revisited. *Journal of Health Politics, Policy and Law*, *13*(2), 239–261.

Felt-Lisk, S., & Higgins, T. (2011, August). *Exploring the promise of population health management programs to improve health* (*Issue brief*). Mathematica Policy Research.

Ferrante, J. M., Balasubramanian, B. A., Hudson, S. V., & Crabtree, B. F. (2010). Principles of the patient-centered medical home and preventive services delivery. *The Annals of Family Medicine*, *8*(2), 108–116.

Friedberg, M. W., Coltin, K. L., Safran, D. G., Dresser, M., & Schneider, E. C. (2010). Medical home capabilities of primary care practices that serve sociodemographically vulnerable neighborhoods. *Archives of Internal Medicine, 170*(11), 938–944.

Glenn, N. D., & Grimes, M. (1968). Aging, voting, and political interest. *American Sociological Review, 33*(4), 563–575.

Goetz Goldberg, D., & Mick, S. S. (2010). Medical home infrastructure: Effect of the environment and practice characteristics on adoption in Virginia. *Medical Care Research and Review, 67*(4), 431–449.

Grumbach, K., & Bodenheimer, T. (2002). A primary care home for Americans: Putting the house in order. *Journal of the American Medical Association, 288*(7), 889–893.

Harrison, D. A., Price, K. H., & Bell, M. P. (1998). Beyond relational demography: Time and the effects of surface- and deep-level diversity on work group cohesion. *Academy of Management Journal, 41*(1), 96–107.

Institute of Medicine. (2003). *Unequal treatment: Confronting racial and ethnic disparities in health care*. Washington, D.C: National Academies Press.

Kane, C. (2009). *The practice arrangements of patient care physicians, 2007–2008: An analysis by age cohort and gender*. Chicago, IL: American Medical Association.

Kaplan, S. H., Gandek, B., Greenfield, S., Rogers, W., & Ware, J. E. (1995). Patient and visit characteristics related to physicians' participatory decision-making style: Results from the medical outcomes study. *Medical Care, 33*(12), 1176–1187.

Levinson, W., Kao, A., Kuby, A., & Thisted, R. A. (2005). Not all patients want to participate in decision making. *Journal of General Internal Medicine, 20*(6), 531–535.

Littell, R., Milliken, G., Stroup, W., & Wolfinger, R. (1996). *SAS system for mixed models*. Cary, NC: SAS Institute, Inc.

Meyer, J. W., & Rowan, B. (1977). Institutionalized organizations: Formal structure as myth and ceremony. *American Journal of Sociology, 83*(2), 340–363.

Nohria, N., & Gulati, R. (1996). Is slack good or bad for innovation? *Academy of Management Journal, 39*(5), 1245–1264.

Nutting, P. A., Crabtree, B. F., Miller, W. L., Stewart, E. E., Stange, K. C., & Jaén, C. R. (2010). Journey to the patient-centered medical home: A qualitative analysis of the experiences of practices in the national demonstration project. *The Annals of Family Medicine, 8*(Suppl. 1), S45–S56.

Nutting, P. A., Miller, W. L., & Crabtree, B. F. (2009). Initial lessons from the first national demonstration project on practice transformation to a patient-centered medical home. *Annals of Family Medicine, 7*(3), 254–260.

Oliver, C. (1991). Strategic responses to institutional processes. *Academy of Management Review, 16*(1), 145–179.

Patient-Centered Primary Care Collaborative. (2009). *Proof in practice. A compilation of patient centered medical home pilot and demonstration projects*. Retrieved from http://www.pcpcc.org/sites/default/files/media/PilotGuidePip.pdf. Accessed on January 14, 2013.

Pfeffer, J., & Salancik, G. R. (1978). *The external control of organizations*. Stanford, CA: Stanford University Press.

Proenca, E. J., Rosko, M. D., & Zinn, J. S. (2000). Correlates of hospital provision of prevention and health promotion services. *Medical Care Research and Review, 60*(1), 58–78.

Raudenbush, S. W., & Bryk, A. S. (2002). *Hierarchical linear models. Applications and data analysis methods*. Thousand Oaks, CA: Sage Publications.

Rich, E. C., Lipson, D., Libersky, J., Peikes, D. N., & Parchman, M. L. (2012). Organizing care for complex patients in the patient-centered medical home. *The Annals of Family Medicine*, *10*(1), 60–62.

Rittenhouse, D. R., Casalino, L. P., Shortell, S. M., McClellan, S. R., Gillies, R. R., Alexander, J. A., & Drum, M. L. (2011). Small and medium-size physician practices use few patient-centered medical home processes. *Health Affairs*, *30*(8), 1575–1584.

Rittenhouse, D. R., & Shortell, S. M. (2009). The patient-centered medical home: Will it stand the test of health reform? *Journal of the American Medical Association*, *301*(19), 2038–2040.

Rittenhouse, D. R., Shortell, S. M., & Fisher, E. S. (2009). Primary care and accountable care – Two essential elements of delivery-system reform. *New England Journal of Medicine*, *361*(24), 2301–2303.

Rogers, E. M. (1995). *Diffusion of innovations* (4th ed.). New York, NY: The Free Press.

Rosenthal, M. B. (2008). Beyond pay for performance – Emerging models of provider-payment reform. *New England Journal of Medicine*, *359*(12), 1197–1200.

Rosenthal, T. C. (2008). The medical home: Growing evidence to support a new approach to primary care. *The Journal of the American Board of Family Medicine*, *21*(5), 427–440.

SAS Institute Inc. (2004). *SAS/STAT user's guide, version 9*. Cary, NC: SAS Institute Inc.

Scott, W. R. (2001). *Institutions and organizations* (2nd ed.).Thousand Oaks, CA: Sage Publishing.

Share, D. A., & Mason, M. H. (2012). Michigan's Physician Group Incentive Program offers a regional model for incremental "fee for value" payment reform. *Health Affairs*, *31*(9), 1993–2001.

Singer, J. D. (1998). Using SAS PROC MIXED to fit multilevel models, hierarchical models, and individual growth models. *Journal of Educational and Behavioral Statistics*, *24*(4), 323–355.

Singer, J. D., & Willett, J. B. (2003). *Applied longitudinal data analysis. Modeling change and event occurrence*. New York, NY: Oxford University Press.

Stange, K., Nutting, P., Miller, W., Jaén, C., Crabtree, B., Flocke, S., & Gill, J. (2010). Defining and measuring the patient-centered medical home. *Journal of General Internal Medicine*, *25*(6), 601–612.

Stiggelbout, A. M., & Kiebert, G. M. (1997). A role for the sick role: Patient preferences regarding information and participation in clinical decision-making. *CMAJ: Canadian Medical Association Journal*, *157*(4), 383–389.

Takach, M. (2012). About half of the states are implementing patient-centered medical homes for their Medicaid populations. *Health Affairs*, *31*(11), 2432–2440.

Uslaner, E. M., & Brown, M. (2005). Inequality, trust, and civic engagement. *American Politics Research*, *33*(6), 868–894.

Walker, R. M. (2007). An empirical evaluation of innovation types and organizational and environmental characteristics: Towards a configuration framework. *Journal of Public Administration Research and Theory*, *18*, 591–615.

Ward, B. W., & Schiller, J. S. (2013). Prevalence of multiple chronic conditions among US adults: Estimates from the National Health Interview Survey, 2010. *Preventing Chronic Disease*, *10*, E65002E.

Wejnert, B. (2002). Integrating models of diffusion of innovations: A conceptual framework. *Annual Review of Sociology*, *28*, 297–329.

Williams, D. R. (1999). Race, socioeconomic status, and health: The added effects of racism and discrimination. *Annals of the New York Academy of Sciences*, *896*(1), 173–188.

Williams, D. R., & Collins, C. (1995). US socioeconomic and racial differences in health: Patterns and explanations. *Annual Review of Sociology*, *21*, 349–386.

Wise, C. G., Alexander, J. A., Green, L. A., Cohen, G. R., & Koster, C. R. (2011). Journey toward a patient-centered medical home: Readiness for change in primary care practices. *Milbank Quarterly*, *89*(3), 399–424.

Zinn, J. S., Weech, R. J., & Brannon, D. (1998). Resource dependence and institutional elements in nursing home TQM adoption. *Health Services Research*, *33*(2 Pt. 1), 261–273.

ENGAGING THE HEALTH CARE TEAM THROUGH OPERATIONS COUNCILS: STRATEGIES TO IMPROVE POPULATION HEALTH FROM WITHIN

Susan Moffatt-Bruce, Ann Scheck McAlearney, Alison Aldrich, Tina Latimer and Edmund Funai

ABSTRACT

Purpose – *Clinical front-line staff are best positioned within the organizations to identify patient safety problems and craft solutions. However, in traditional models, safety committees are led by senior executives who are not clinically responsible for patients. This top-down approach can result in missed opportunities to address patient-centered challenges and better manage the health of the defined populations served by these organizations.*

Design/methodology/approach – *To foster teamwork, enhance empowerment, and improve the patient care environment, Operations Councils led by trained front-line staff were deployed in 15 clinical areas*

Population Health Management in Health Care Organizations
Advances in Health Care Management, Volume 16, 51–67

ISSN: 1474-8231/doi:10.1108/S1474-823120140000016003

at the Ohio State University Wexner Medical Center (OSUWMC) as a performance improvement tool.

Findings – *Standardized training of Council facilitators was designed and implemented to guide the performance improvement process. Balanced scorecards were developed in each Council based on the risks and concerns of that particular clinical area. After initial implementation of the Operations Councils, patient safety events declined and team engagement improved by over 34% across the medical center; the highest changes were seen in areas where Operations Councils had been deployed. Additionally, outcome metrics including area-specific and system-wide mortality and readmissions improved after implementation.*

Originality/value – *We suggest that this type of approach may be an appropriate strategy to consider in other health care organizations as such institutions are challenged to better manage the health of their defined patient populations.*

Keywords: Patient safety; hospital management; performance improvement

INTRODUCTION

Comprehensive population health management strategies implemented by health systems or insurers must coordinate care provision and management with hospitals and health care organizations that care for increasingly complex patients. Within such institutions, an important element of care management involves continuous monitoring and evaluation of quality of care, patient safety, and efficiency. Health care leaders, as a result, are searching for viable options to cut costs and increase efficiencies while still providing highly reliable and sound medical care. Yet there is no standard way of achieving "value" in such environments, leading to the introduction and adoption of different approaches to performance, process, and quality improvement.

Management techniques from business and industry including Lean, Six Sigma, and the Toyota Production System (TPS) have often been studied in relation to health care process improvement (Kim, Spahlinger, Kin, & Billi, 2006; Mazzocato, Savage, Brommels, Aronsson, & Thor, 2010; Robbins, Garman, Song, & McAlearney, 2012; Teich & Faddoul, 2013;

Young & McClean, 2008). These techniques share common foundations such as maintaining respect for people and focusing on continuous improvement. But across approaches there also exists a tension between medical and business approaches to process improvement (Alexander & Hearld, 2009; Andersen, Rovik, & Ingebrigtsen, 2014; Walshe, 2007). In practice, Lean and other process improvement methodologies must take into account the context and environments in which they are applied, with long-term success only possible if organizations can change behaviorally and culturally to embrace a focus on continuous improvement.

As a performance improvement process, for example, Lean philosophy calls for value creation through elimination of waste. These wastes are common in all industries and perhaps are most evident in health care (Bush, 2007; Manos, Sattler, & Alukal, 2006). Much of the waste can be detected by front-line workers without specific training in process improvement. Institutions, however, must trust and empower health care workers to find waste, and have the discipline necessary to implement waste reduction strategies when waste is identified. Health systems have had success engaging front-line workers in process improvement. For example, in 2001, Virginia Mason Medical Center (VMMC) focused on engaging leaders and front-line staff in rapid process improvement workshops (RPIW); this involved an intensive focus on improving processes identified as broken or defective (Nelson-Peterson & Leppa, 2007). Front-line engagement has also led to successful process improvement efforts in pediatric intensive care settings (Vats et al., 2012) and in highly specialized total joint replacement care pathways (Van Citters et al., 2014). A key element in the success of these initiatives is the engagement of front-line staff who understand the processes and of leaders who can lead the change.

In traditional health care organizations, however, responsibility and accountability for patient safety, patient satisfaction, staff satisfaction, and operational efficiency have resided with senior leaders who are not clinically responsible for the patients. For example, the Institute for Healthcare Improvement (IHI) and other organizations promote the practice of "patient safety walk rounds" whereby leaders identify specific patient safety problems and promote a culture of safety (Frankel et al., 2008; Rotteau, Shojania, & Webster, 2014). However, these walk rounds can fail to facilitate improvements in direct patient care because the leaders may not be viewed as a part of the team (Rotteau et al., 2014). We propose a more bottom-up, grassroots approach that engages those on the front lines of health care to identify challenges, implement solutions, and sustain change in the areas of quality, patient safety, resource utilization, patient experience, and financial responsibility.

As performance and quality improvement are important elements of all population health management approaches, we sought to explore how a performance improvement strategy focused on patient safety improvement could be developed and deployed in a large academic medical center. Specifically, we investigated whether the creation and implementation of Operations Councils, defined as regularly meeting teams comprised of clinical front-line staff, could increase patient safety and improve the health of the hospitalized patient population by improving the patient care environment and the hospital's organizational culture. These councils are an extension of the process improvement models discussed above, such as Lean, because they employ traditional process improvement techniques with a focus on building a collaborative culture that incorporates front-line staff in the process.

METHODS

Study Setting

Based in the Midwest, the Ohio State University Wexner Medical Center (OSUWMC) has over 57,000 admissions every year. As one of the largest and most diverse academic medical centers in the country and central Ohio's only academic medical center, OSWMC includes a top-ranked College of Medicine; six hospitals; a unified physician practice; a network of primary and specialty care practices; more than a dozen research centers and institutes; and 20 core laboratories.

As a health care system striving to improve population health from within, we aimed to foster a culture of empowerment for the employees who know our patients best and, in so doing, to improve patient safety and overall patient satisfaction. We borrowed heavily from Lean process improvement techniques relative to the principles of identifying high-risk clinical areas, engaging front-line staff, facilitating process change and continuously looking toward improvement. We implemented Operations Councils in a cyclical plan-do-study-act (PDSA) approach to quality improvement (Kovner & Rundall, 2005), as we describe further below.

Planning: Baseline Data

Every two years, employees across the OSUWMC complete the Culture of Safety survey from the Agency for Healthcare Research and Quality (AHRQ). Survey results reviewed over time (see Table 1) revealed considerable and consistent opportunities for improvement in 2007, 2009, and 2011. In particular, teamwork within units and communication failures were identified as areas that needed to be addressed.

Doing: Crew Resource Management (CRM) Initiative

Based on the early rounds of AHRQ Safety Culture survey results and the desire to improve as an organization, OSUWMC established a partnership with LifeWings Partners LLC to provide crew resource management (CRM) training. As a first step, a team of LifeWings consultants including Air Force and naval aviators, astronauts, and professional pilots conducted observations in several units across the OSUWMC health system. Their assessment included measurements of inter-professional collaboration and communication; standardization of processes within a given business unit and between business units; and signs of normalization of deviation from expected practices. The consultants then created an implementation and training plan based on engagement and readiness; staff and patient satisfaction; sentinel event and safety climate data. Since December 2010, over 4000 physicians, nurses, staff, and administrators have undergone the standardized team training associated with CRM.

Studying: Results of CRM Training

Our evaluation of the CRM program provided considerable insight about our employees' capabilities and our ability to be resilient as a health system (Moffatt-Bruce & Ellison, 2012; Moffatt-Bruce, Funai, Nash, & Gabbe, 2012). We found that our experience was similar to that seen in other academic medical centers, particularly around obstetrical services (Pettker et al., 2011). However, completion of the CRM training was only a first step. Addressing employees' and clinical areas' abilities to communicate among themselves enabled us to explore the concept of Operations Councils, an approach that depended upon mutual respect and inter-professional collaboration to succeed.

Table 1. Agency for Health Care Research and Quality (AHRQ) Safety Culture Survey Results, 2007, 2009, 2011 for Ohio State University Wexler Medical Center.

Category	OSUWMC (2007) (%)	Ranking (All Hosp.)	OSUWMC (2009) (%)	Ranking (All Hosp.)	OSUWMC (2011) (%)	Ranking (All Hosp.)	National Top Decile (%)
Teamwork within units	73.7	10th percentile	78.1	25th percentile	76.4	25th percentile	87
Supervisor expectations	66.9	10th percentile	72.1	25th percentile	69.4	10th percentile	83
Management support for patient safety	59.1	10th percentile	68.0	25th percentile	65.6	10th percentile	84
Organizational learning	63.9	10th percentile	71.0	25th percentile	65.6	10th percentile	82
Overall perception of patient safety	56.8	10th percentile	62.7	25th percentile	59.6	10th percentile	76
Feedback about errors	50.9	Bottom decile	56.8	10th percentile	53.7	Bottom decile	75

Acting: Establishing Operations Councils

Introducing the Concept

In 2012, the concept of Operations Councils was introduced to senior leadership and described as a grassroots approach to managing the changing and increasingly complex patient population across the continuum of care at OSUWMC. Senior leadership agreed to adopt the Operations Council model, and defined three criteria upon which clinical areas would be evaluated with respect to their need for an Operations Council: (1) the occurrence of a serious patient safety event in the past 12 months; (2) engaged nurses, physicians, and administrators trained in crew resource management; and (3) a defined patient population (e.g., patients with chronic conditions). Based on these criteria, five clinical areas were initially targeted for Operations Councils: neonatal services, obstetrical services, emergency department, cardiovascular service lines, and orthopedic surgery. However, because the area of cardiovascular services was itself multi-disciplinary, this area was further divided into electrophysiology, vascular surgery, open heart surgery, invasive cardiology, heart failure, ambulatory cardiac services, and perioperative cardiac services. As a result, 10 Operations Councils were initiated in September 2012. Later, in March 2013, Operations Councils were established for radiology, interventional radiology, medical intensive care services and perioperative services, creating a total of 15 Operations Councils across OSUWMC.

Composition of Operations Councils

Each of the 15 Operations Councils was led by a team of one physician, one nurse, and one administrator, and included approximately 10–12 front-line staff. In addition, each Operations Council identified one of their front-line staff members to be a dedicated facilitator and receive preliminary training in Lean and Six Sigma methodologies. The Operations Councils initially met weekly in order to promote team development and enable the teams to develop a problem focus. In addition, while the groups were being formed, the OSUWMC Chief Quality and Patient Safety Officer and the Chief Operating Officer met with every Operations Council to provide further support and to help define Council structure and function.

Operations Councils Vision and Mission

The *vision* of the Operations Councils was to provide a safe experience and environment for all patients. This was to be accomplished through open and transparent communication, team training, a core team of leaders, and a facility that enhanced patient flow through efficient and timely care delivery. The *mission* of the OSUWMC Operations Councils was to optimize patient safety, improve patient outcomes and satisfaction, and ultimately to create a working environment that was more enjoyable for all staff and providers. Additionally, the Operations Council members had a duty to each other to accomplish this with mutual respect, support, and enthusiasm. In Operations Councils, there was a need to focus on how individuals and teams could contribute to improving the environment. All team members were to refrain from giving reasons why change was impossible.

Standardized Training of Operations Council Facilitators
Each Operations Council was charged to select one of their front-line staff members to be the Council facilitator. This individual needed to be able to dedicate time to be trained as a Lean Six Sigma facilitator while also staying clinically active. Across Councils, designated facilitators were nurses, pharmacists, and technicians. The role of the facilitator was to assist the Operations Council team with work plan development, adhering to timelines, structuring work rounds and/or facilitated meetings, developing the project team charter, and improving performance overall. The facilitators met monthly with the Chief Quality and Patient Safety Officer and the Executive Director of Quality and Operations, both experts in Lean Six Sigma and process improvement. During those sessions, the facilitators shared information about their current projects with the other Operations Council facilitators and discussed challenges and successes. The facilitators also completed Lean Six Sigma yellow belt training through Ohio State University's Fisher College of Business in their first year of Operations Council deployment. Each facilitator was paired with a coach within the health system for ongoing support and assistance with project development. These coaches were all experienced health care process improvement experts.

Development of Operations Council Scorecards
Each Operations Council met initially to brainstorm about problems in their area that they would attempt to solve, and then worked to develop a balanced scorecard specific to that area and the problems to be addressed. All outcome and process metrics selected by the Operations Councils were to be in alignment with the health system's designated key result areas of innovation and strategic growth, productivity and efficiency, quality, and service and reputation, and be targeted to monitor the problems they were addressing. The Emergency Department Operations Council, for example,

Table 2. Emergency Department Operations Council Scorecard.

Key Results Area	FY12 Actual	FY13 Target	FY13 Actual
Innovation and strategic growth			
ED volume	Feb-12 5,597 Mar-12 6,150 Apr-12 6,152 FY12 YTD – 59,334	Feb-13 5,947 Mar-13 6,029 Apr-13 6,059 FY13 YTD – 60,089 (Budget)	Feb-13 5,144 Mar-13 5,549 Apr-13 5,838 FY13 YTD – 57,022
Inpatient admissions including observations	Feb-12 1,547 Mar-12 1,691 Apr-12 1,577 FY12 YTD – 15,727	Feb-13 1,567 Mar-13 1,588 Apr-13 1,596 FY13 YTD – 15,830 (Budget)	Feb-13 1,516 Mar-13 1,684 Apr-13 1,709 FY13 YTD – 16,502
Productivity and efficiency			
Length of stay – all patients (wo CDU observation)	Feb-12 5.95 hours Mar-12 5.98 hours Apr-12 5.66 hours FY12 YTD – 5.72 hours	FY13– 4.05 hours (UHC Top Quartile Benchmark)	Feb-13 6.06 hours Mar-13 5.72 hours Apr-13 5.72 hours FY13 YTD – 5.90 hours
Length of stay – admitted patients (wo CDU observation)	Feb-12 7.75 hours Mar-12 8.70 hours Apr-12 8.28 hours FY12 YTD – 8.13 hours	FY13 – 5.58 hours (UHC Top Quartile Benchmark)	Feb-13 8.44 hours Mar-13 7.92 hours Apr-13 7.70 hours FY13 YTD – 8.28 hours
Length of stay – discharged (main ED and fast track wo CDU observation)	Feb-12 4.92 hours Mar-12 4.74 hours Apr-12 4.42 hours FY12 YTD – 4.60 hours	FY13 – 3.40 hours (UHC Top Quartile Benchmark)	Feb-13 4.76 hours Mar-13 4.54 hours Apr-13 4.73 hours FY13 YTD – 4.75 hours
Quality			
Left without being seen	Feb-12 4.40% Mar-12 4.80% Apr-12 4.13% FY12 YTD – 4.11%	FY13 – 1.7% (UHC Top Quartile Benchmark)	Feb-13 3.11% Mar-13 3.15% Apr-13 3.82% FY13 YTD 3.49%

Table 2. *(Continued)*

Key Results Area	FY12 Actual	FY13 Target	FY13 Actual
Service and reputation			
Patient satisfaction	Jan-12 78.7% Feb-12 78.4% Mar-12 79.5% FY12 – 79.2%	FY13 – 86.6%	Jan-13 80.4% Feb-13 79.1% Mar-13 79.9% FY13 YTD – 80.4%

Table 3. Invasive Cardiology Operations Council Scorecard.

Leadership council for clinical quality, safety, and service goals FY 2013	
Quality and safety	Reduce overall quality and safety Scorecard events by 25% Focus areas: Falls, DPPUs, SSI, Clostridium difficile reduction Improve in risk adjusted inpatient mortality domain for ross quality and accountability study to index ≤0.9 Achieve top decile in all value-based purchasing clinical indicators Hand hygiene compliance of ≥90%
Productivity and efficiency	Achieve 25% reduction in all cause admission rate Improve inpatient capacity Peak occupancy rate (≤85%) O/E length of stay (≤1.0) Discharge orders placed by 10 AM (≥50%)
Service and reputation	Achieve top decile status for patient satisfaction HCAHPS score ≥83.5%
Operations council quality and safety scorecard	
Type of event	FY10 to FY12 2 year change
Medication errors with harm (severity E–I)	−81%
Falls with harm (injury level 2–4)	+200%
Hospital-acquired pressure ulcer	+32%
Central line bloodstream infection	−81%
Ventilator-associated pneumonia	−50%
Hospital-acquired C. Difficile	+107%

developed a scorecard that encompassed publicly reported metrics as well as metrics that were in alignment with the health system's priorities (Table 2). Similarly, the Invasive Cardiology and the Open Heart Operations Councils developed scorecards that were inclusive of metrics that could be derived from registry data, but also permitted sharing of information such as acute myocardial infarction indicators, heart failure discharge instructions, and pneumonia measures that was felt to be important and motivating to front-line staff (Table 3). The Invasive Cardiology Operations Council scorecards aligned their metrics with the health system goals.

Data Collection and Reporting

Data were provided to the Operations Council facilitators on a monthly basis, with analytic support provided by the health system's Quality and Operations department. The facilitators were also required to report their results at regular retreats attended by OSUWMC senior leadership. Some of the Operations Councils additionally developed newsletters and websites that allowed for broader sharing of data and improvements (e.g., http://u.osu.edu/cardiacsurgeryops/). At an organizational level, OSUWMC also monitored data and maintained scorecards reporting outcomes on a regular basis. For instance, the Patient Safety Scorecard (Fig. 1) was developed to monitor overall patient safety across the institution, with activities of individual Operations Councils supporting the institutional goal of patient safety improvement.

Quality and Safety Scorecard

Type of Event
Retained Foreign Bodies
Wrong procedure/site/person events
Medication Events with Harm (Severity E-I)
Severe Injury Falls (Resulting in Change in Patient Outcome)
Hospital Acquired Decubitus Ulcer
Central Line Blood Stream Infections
Ventilator Associated Pneumonia
Hospital Acquired Surgical Site Infections
Hospital Acquired Clostridium Difficile Infection
Total Potentially Avoidable Events

Fig. 1. OSUWMC Patient Safety Scorecard.

RESULTS

The implementation of Operations Councils across OSUWMC has had both area-specific and institution-wide impact. One area-specific example involved an Operations Council formed at the OSUWMC's community hospital to address perioperative issues. The Perioperative Operations Council decided to focus on the problems of on-time starts for surgeries and turnover time for operating rooms. Each of these topics required the Councils to address performance issues around employee engagement and communication that could impact the scorecard metrics. During the initial measurement phase, the Operations Council focused on identifying the reasons for delays in start times and operating room turnover, and attempted to pinpoint responsibility for these delays. By distinguishing between surgeon-related and staff-related delays, for instance, the team could further drill down into these issues and uncover opportunities to address factors under their control. In only eight months the Perioperative Operations Council was able to report dramatic improvements, with on-time starts increasing to 80% from a low of 35% (Fig. 2).

A second example of area-specific improvements involved the OSUWMC's Heart Hospital in the area of ambulatory care. The Ross Ambulatory Operations Council was formed to focus primarily on clinic

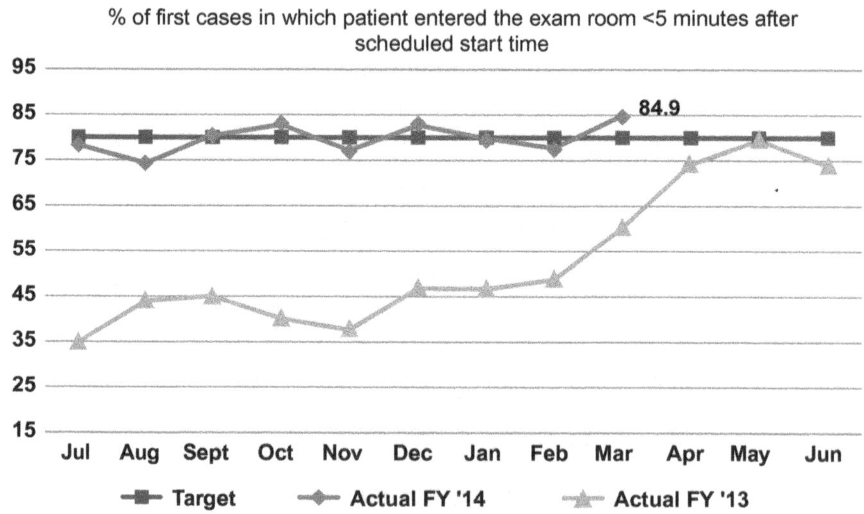

Fig. 2. OSU East First On-Time Starts.

visits for patients after they had been hospitalized, recognizing that these patients often needed follow-up appointments with a cardiologist, a vascular specialist, or a surgeon. Upon review of data from both staff and patient satisfaction surveys, the Operations Council identified the need to reduce waiting times for patients undergoing stress echocardiogram tests. Contributing to long waiting times were both factors that could not be controlled (e.g., the patient was late) and those that could (e.g., waiting for the nurse, waiting for the physician). A major factor identified involved waiting for the sonographer. The Operations Council was then able to address the factors that could be controlled, including training a new sonographer to help reduce that barrier. As a result, waiting times for patients undergoing stress echocardiograms dropped drastically in less than a year (Fig. 3).

Operations Councils also impacted the entire organization in a number of ways. Three areas of particular focus were patient safety, readmissions, and patient satisfaction, all of which require dedicated employee engagement to ensure improvement. In examining impact on patient safety, we recognized that the notion of avoidable harm to patients differs depending where the patient is and what type of diagnosis they carry. For instance, for the Cardiovascular Operations Councils, there was a tremendous focus on medication safety and perioperative processes. Through the Council processes they formulated standards around the use of anti-platelet

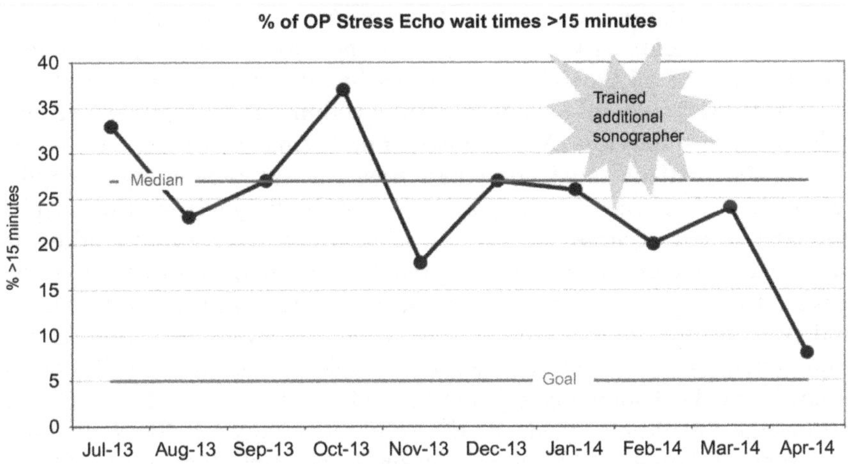

Fig. 3. Ross Ambulatory Operations Council: Reducing Wait Times for Outpatient Stress Echocardiograms.

drugs for patients undergoing procedures that involved coronary stents. Interestingly, this effort to keep cardiology patients safe after stent placement then expanded to a medical center-wide standard. Similarly, the focus on reducing catheter-associated urinary tract infections (CAUTIs) among patients in the medical intensive care unit became a system-wide initiative. While the CAUTI-reduction strategies used in the medical ICU were very different from those in the surgical ICU, the patient safety focus and prevention goals were the same. Institution-wide, OSUWMC credits Operations Councils with reductions in both medication harm events and mortality among patients who arrived with life-threatening cardiovascular emergencies, contributing to a 22% reduction in patient safety events across the entire medical center over the past two years.

Reducing readmission rates was targeted as another institutional goal for OSUWMC and a focus of most Operations Councils. For the Cardiovascular Operations Councils, the readmissions associated with heart failure, acute myocardial infarction, and pneumonia were of particular concern. Given the Operations Council performance improvement approach of identifying problems and then exploring solutions, we found that different Councils implemented different solutions as appropriate for their clinical areas and the needs of the particular patient population they served. Solutions ranged from expanding outreach at discharge to include discharge phone calls to introducing patient navigators to help patients stay out of the hospital. Results from these efforts have shown a reduction in all-cause readmissions by approximately 16% over the past two years.

Finally, patient satisfaction was identified as an important indicator for the focus of all Operations Councils because it was a key result area for OSUWMC and of high importance within the Center for Medicare and Medicaid Services Value-Based Purchasing program. Across the OSUWMC, patient satisfaction had been measured monthly, compiling results from surveys sent to patients after discharge from the hospital. Similar to what occurred in the case of focusing on reducing readmission rates, each Operations Council approached the patient satisfaction challenge differently depending on the issues they saw within their own area and given their particular patient population. For example, within the neonatal intensive care unit, the solution implemented by that Operations Council involved allowing the mother full access to her baby. For the orthopedic Operations Council, the solution involved a focus on timely outpatient follow-up. At an institution level, each Operations Council initiative has likely contributed to improvements in overall patient satisfaction scores, and, as a result, has improved the metrics upon which value-based purchasing is based.

DISCUSSION

The direct impact of Operations Councils on the health of our patient population is difficult to measure. How do you measure success of a grass roots process improvement strategy that is more about changing a culture than actually moving the needle on a specific metric? At a time when most organizations have multiple initiatives underway to improve overall quality, no clear statistical method is able to fully isolate the impact of one particular approach.

We have tried to measure our successes relative to cultural changes and perception. For instance, as part of patient safety surveys, we have been able to discern that we still need to be more transparent with data. To that end, the newsletters and the websites the Operations Councils have developed have become increasingly populated with sensitive and meaningful data. They remain behind the institutional firewall, but will serve ultimately as a testament to our commitment to transparency as an institution.

In an era of trying to do more with less, the ability to affect change is difficult. Readmissions are a key area of focus for both state and federal process improvement efforts, making this a clear priority for health care organizations. Similarly, the ability to discharge patients appropriately and have them continue their care in the outpatient arena is paramount to the patient experience across institutions.

At the OSUWMC the Operations Councils have been formulated and supported so that the needs of different patient populations could be addressed and the changes sustained by the people at the front lines who know these needs best. We intend to expand the number and scope of the Operations Councils to affect change amongst a larger number of patient populations. In order to be able to do that, we will need continued support from physicians, nurses, and administration. Data metrics are key to driving and measuring improvements, but sustainability remains a challenge. As key personnel changes in areas are inevitable over time, hardwiring of successful processes is of utmost importance. Having the front-line staff engaged should lend itself to improved patient and staff satisfaction. If ever there was a time to embrace a grassroots approach to continuous improvement, it is now.

REFERENCES

Alexander, J. A., & Hearld, L. R. (2009). What can we learn from quality improvement research? A critical review of research methods. *Medical Care Research and Review: MCRR*, *66*(3), 235–271. doi:10.1177/1077558708330424

Andersen, H., Rovik, K. A., & Ingebrigtsen, T. (2014). Lean thinking in hospitals: Is there a cure for the absence of evidence? A systematic review of reviews. *BMJ Open*, *4*(1), 1–8. doi:10.1136/bmjopen-2013-003873

Bush, R. W. (2007). Reducing waste in US health care systems. *JAMA: The Journal of the American Medical Association*, 297(8), 871–874. doi:10.1001/jama.297.8.871

Frankel, A., Grillo, S. P., Pittman, M., Thomas, E. J., Horowitz, L., Page, M., & Sexton, B. (2008). Revealing and resolving patient safety defects: The impact of leadership walk-rounds on front line caregiver assessments of patient safety. *Health Services Research*, *43*(6), 2050–2066. doi:10.1111/j.1475-6773.2008.00878.x

Kim, C. S., Spahlinger, D. A., Kin, J. M., & Billi, J. E. (2006). Lean health care: What can hospitals learn from a world-class automaker? *Journal of Hospital Medicine: An Official Publication of the Society of Hospital Medicine*, *1*(3), 191–199. doi:10.1002/jhm.68

Kovner, A. R., & Rundall, T. (2005). Evidence-based management reconsidered. *Frontiers of Health Services Management*, *22*(3), 3–22.

Manos, A., Sattler, M., & Alukal, G. (2006). Make healthcare lean. *Quality Progress*, *39*, 24–29.

Mazzocato, P., Savage, C., Brommels, M., Aronsson, H., & Thor, J. (2010). Lean thinking in healthcare: A realist review of the literature. *Quality & Safety in Health Care*, *19*(5), 376–382. doi:10.1136/qshc.2009.037986

Moffatt-Bruce, S. D., & Ellison, E. C. (2012). Celebrating human resilience to provide safe care. *Annals of Surgery*, *256*(2), 211–212. doi:10.1097/SLA.0b013e3182602565

Moffatt-Bruce, S. D., Funai, E. F., Nash, M., & Gabbe, S. G. (2012). Patient safety strategies: Are we on the same team? *Obstetrics and Gynecology*, *120*(4), 743–745. doi:10.1097/AOG.0b013e31826af730

Nelson-Peterson, D. L., & Leppa, C. J. (2007). Creating an environment for caring using lean principles of the Virginia mason production system. *The Journal of Nursing Administration*, *37*(6), 287–294. doi:10.1097/01.NNA.0000277717.34134.a9

Pettker, C. M., Thung, S. F., Raab, C. A., Donohue, K. P., Copel, J. A., Lockwood, C. J., & Funai, E. F. (2011). A comprehensive obstetrics patient safety program improves safety climate and culture. *American Journal of Obstetrics and Gynecology*, *204*(3), 216.e1–216.e6. doi:10.1016/j.ajog.2010.11.004

Robbins, J., Garman, A. N., Song, P. H., & McAlearney, A. S. (2012). How high-performance work systems drive health care value: An examination of leading process improvement strategies. *Quality Management in Health Care*, *21*(3), 188–202. doi:10.1097/QMH.0b013e31825e88f6

Rotteau, L., Shojania, K. G., & Webster, F. (2014). 'I think we should just listen and get out': A qualitative exploration of views and experiences of patient safety walkrounds. *BMJ Quality & Safety*, Jan 9. doi:10.1136/bmjqs-2012-001706 [Epub ahead of print].

Teich, S. T., & Faddoul, F. F. (2013). Lean management – The journey from Toyota to healthcare. *Rambam Maimonides Medical Journal*, *4*(2), e0007. doi:10.5041/RMMJ.10107

Van Citters, A. D., Fahlman, C., Goldmann, D. A., Lieberman, J. R., Koenig, K. M., Digioia, A. M., 3rd, … Bozic, K. J. (2014). Developing a pathway for high-value, patient-centered total joint arthroplasty. *Clinical Orthopaedics and Related Research*, *472*(5), 1619–1635. doi:10.1007/s11999-013-3398-4

Vats, A., Goin, K. H., Villarreal, M. C., Yilmaz, T., Fortenberry, J. D., & Keskinocak, P. (2012). The impact of a lean rounding process in a pediatric intensive care unit. *Critical Care Medicine*, *40*(2), 608–617. doi:10.1097/CCM.0b013e318232e2fc

Walshe, K. (2007). Understanding what works – and why – in quality improvement: The need for theory-driven evaluation. *International Journal for Quality in Health Care: Journal of the International Society for Quality in Health Care/ISQua, 19*(2), 57–59. doi:10.1093/intqhc/mzm004

Young, T. P., & McClean, S. I. (2008). A critical look at lean thinking in healthcare. *Quality & Safety in Health Care, 17*(5), 382–386. doi:10.1136/qshc.2006.020131

SECTION II
PHM BETWEEN HEALTH CARE ORGANIZATIONS

USING TEAMS TO IMPLEMENT PERSONALIZED HEALTH CARE ACROSS A MULTI-SITE BREAST CANCER NETWORK

Sarah Lewis, Joan Bloom, Jennifer Rice, Arash Naeim and Stephen Shortell

ABSTRACT

Purpose – *This study sought to identify the organizational factors associated with team and network effectiveness of the Athena Breast Health Network, a multi-site collaboration between five University of California health systems.*

Design/methodology/approach – *Providers, managers, and support staff completed self-administered surveys over three years. Statistical analyses at the network and medical center levels tested hypotheses regarding the correlates of effective teams and perceived network effectiveness over time.*

Findings – *Perceived team effectiveness was positively correlated with group culture and environments which support collaboration, negatively correlated with hierarchical culture, and negatively associated with*

Population Health Management in Health Care Organizations
Advances in Health Care Management, Volume 16, 71–94

ISSN: 1474-8231/doi:10.1108/S1474-823120140000016004

professional tenure at year two. As measured by increasing team effectiveness scores over time and Athena's potential impact on patient care, perceived network effectiveness was positively associated with team effectiveness.

Research limitations/implications – *Results do not allow us to conclude that a certain type of culture "causes" team effectiveness or that team effectiveness "causes" greater perceptions of progress over time. Subsequent studies should examine these variables simultaneously. Further research is needed to examine the role of payment incentives, internal reward systems, the use of electronic health records, public disclosure of performance data, and depth of leadership within each organization and within the network overall.*

Practical implications – *Focusing on group affiliation and participation may improve team member perceptions regarding effectiveness and impact on patient care.*

Originality/value – *Relatively little is known about the adaptive processes that occur within inter-organizational networks to achieve desired goals, and particularly the roles played by multi-disciplinary interprofessional teams. We studied a network comprising multiple campuses actively involved in better understanding, preventing, and treating a complex disease.*

Keywords: Network; team effectiveness; organizational culture; multidisciplinary

INTRODUCTION

Health care reform is causing turbulent changes in the environment of all health care organizations. The "Triple Aim" of the Patient Protection and Affordable Care Act (ACA) to reduce costs, increase access, and improve quality of care has pushed changing payment and delivery models within the health care system (Whitehouse, 2012). Ongoing implementation of ACA provisions related to delivery system redesign such as accountable care organizations and patient-centered medical homes reflect the trend of moving away from fragmented care and toward integrated, team-based care. Amid these reforms, one developing trend is the continued growth of mergers and alliances among hospitals and health systems and inter-organizational networks of various forms.

In an alliance, two or more independent organizations coordinate activities and/or share knowledge or resources in the pursuit of a common set of objectives (Scott, 2003). In contrast to traditional hierarchical inter-organizational relationships or mergers, collaborative arrangements such as networks offer greater flexibility for participants due to more limited involvement as well as more opportunities to provide complementary skills (Powell, 1987). Combining strengths and working across functional levels to leverage "know-how" located outside a single organization's boundaries implies mutually beneficial, interdependent relationships.

It comes as no surprise, then, that one way in which inter-organizational networks achieve some degree of success is through the development of multi-disciplinary inter-professional teams that are used to develop shared goals and objectives, knowledge, information, and support that facilitate achievement of network objectives. In any complex health care delivery setting "a large number of professionals with diverse expertise must work together" (Valentine, Nembhard, & Edmondson, 2011); in a network, multi-disciplinary teamwork within and across organizations assumes even greater importance. Researchers have called for greater attention to context in the design of teamwork studies. Yet, despite the proliferation of inter-organizational networks, relatively little is known about the adaptive processes that occur within such networks to achieve the desired goals of network formation and, in particular, the roles played by multi-disciplinary inter-professional teams.

Reflecting the above-mentioned definition of a network, a team is "a collection of individuals who are interdependent in their tasks, who share responsibility for outcomes, who see themselves and who are seen by others as an intact social entity embedded in one or more larger social systems, and who manage their relationships across organizational boundaries" (Cohen & Bailey, 1997; Lemieux-Charles & McGuire, 2006).

We had a unique opportunity to study the birth and early development over time of an academic clinical research and inter-organizational patient care network associated with five University of California medical centers. Given the obstacles to collaboration engendered by organizational boundaries and identities (Gittell & Weiss, 2004), the present study aims to answer the question: what influences perceived effectiveness in a multi-site clinical research environment? We contribute to the organizational studies and health care teamwork literature by studying a network comprising multiple campuses actively involved in better understanding, preventing, and treating a complex disease. The research design allows us to not only identify relationships between effectiveness and related organizational variables in the context of a multi-site collaboration, but also describe how perceptions of participation in the network have evolved over time.

ORGANIZING FRAMEWORK AND HYPOTHESES

As shown in Fig. 1, we hypothesize that more effective teams are associated with greater perceived network effectiveness, and that certain team-level processes and contextual factors are associated with more effective teams.

Perceived team effectiveness is "the extent to which a team feels it has the necessary information, authority, autonomy, and related items to do its work" (Cretin, Shortell, & Keeler, 2004). A positive workplace climate motivates staff and teams to work together effectively, which in turn allows for system changes to be implemented, leading to improved care processes for individual patients and ultimately, patient outcomes. According to Vinokur-Kaplan's (1995) conceptual model of team effectiveness, "enabling group conditions" such as effort, amount of knowledge and skill applied to work, and appropriateness of strategies mediate the effect of initial conditions – team size, task clarity, feelings of influence on teammates, availability of consultation, and environmental support – on team effectiveness.

In addition to measures of self-assessed technical quality as conceptualized by Cretin et al, the extent to which teams positively perceive task outcomes and believe that their team's performance met their expectations

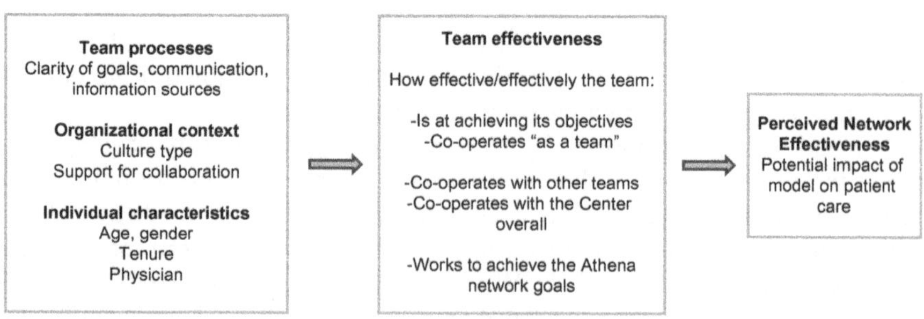

Fig. 1. Conceptual Model of Team Effectiveness in a Multi-Site Clinical Collaboration.

add to the team effectiveness concept (Lemieux-Charles & McGuire, 2006). According to the Integrated Team Effectiveness Model (ITEM), effectiveness is directly influenced by team processes such as communication, team psycho-social traits such as cohesion, and task design (Table 1). Elements of task design – composed of task type, task features, and team composition – also influence team processes and traits.

Task-related characteristics such as task clarity and clarity of goals and objectives have been correlated with team effectiveness in health care settings (Poulton & West, 1999). At the team level, effectiveness is associated with commitment to team objectives (Poulton & West, 1999), shared beliefs regarding team efficacy (Edmonson, 1999), and effective communication (Shortell, Rousseau, Gillies, Devers, & Simons, 1991; Temkin-Greener, Gross, Kunitz, & Mukamel, 2004). Elements associated with the successful operation of a multi-year, multi-center clinical cancer research network include shared vision and regular and effective communication (Hagen et al., 2011).

Under the organizational context domain of the ITEM, emphasis on quality and quality improvement practices, an environment amenable to collaboration, and support for innovation have shown to be positively associated with team effectiveness (Lemieux-Charles et al., 2002; Poulton & West, 1999). An organization's emphasis on elements such as resources and rewards is posited to exert an indirect influence on effectiveness through the team-level factors mentioned above. Goal attainment and efficiency, innovation, rules and regulations, and/or meeting people's needs for affiliation can all be emphasized in relatively different degrees (Quinn & Kimberly, 1984). Many of these concepts are captured by the competing values framework for examining organizational culture (Zammuto & Krakower, 1991). This framework highlights four value types: (1) group culture is based on norms and values associated with affiliation, teamwork, and participation; (2) developmental culture is based on risk-taking, innovation, and change; (3) hierarchical culture reflects the values and norms associated with bureaucracy; and (4) rational culture emphasizes efficiency and achievement (Nembhard, Singer, Shortell, Rittenhouse, & Casalino, 2012). Every organization will have elements of all four types; in fact some studies suggest that a more balanced culture across all four types is positively associated with perceived team effectiveness (Shortell et al., 2004). Group and developmental culture types have also been significantly associated with team effectiveness (Howard, Brazil, Akhtar-Danesh, & Agarwal, 2011) as have patient-centered and team-satisfaction oriented organizational culture (Edmonson, 1999; Nembhard et al., 2012).

Table 1. Synthesis of Determinants of Team Effectiveness by Integrated Health Care Team Effectiveness (ITEM) Domains.

Study	Team Effectiveness Measure	Team Setting	Independent Variables		
			Organizational factors/ context	Task features and processes	Team composition
Hospital or hospital unit					
Shortell et al. (2004)	8-item scale of overall team effectiveness Three 5-item scales: Team skill Participation and goal agreement Organizational support	40 collaborative care management teams at 40 sites	**Culture**: **balance** (across four types) and *patient-centered* *Commitment to QI* (focus on patient satisfaction) Presence of team champion	n/a	Team size Discipline: **involvement of physicians** Disease focus (e.g., asthma)
Lemieux-Charles et al. (2002)	Four 5-point scales of perceived effectiveness	97 cross-functional acute care teams at 11 acute care and teaching hospitals with 100 + beds	Implementation of key QI principles and tools *Supportive environment for QI practices* Establishment of norms	Internal management processes: Established group norms *Follow group process strategies* Engaged in well-designed decision-making practices	n/a
Vinokur-Kaplan (1995)	Standards met, cohesion, well-being and overall effectiveness	15 multi-disciplinary teams at 3 psychiatric hospitals	Physical environment for meeting **Supportive organizational environment**	Group interdependence Interdisciplinary collaboration Task clarity *Feelings of influence on teammates*	Team size
Shortell et al. (1991)	Unit effectiveness: Perceived effectiveness of technical quality and meeting family member needs, and nurse turnover	26 teams and top management at medical/ surgical ICUs	Org. culture inventory: *Team satisfaction* People security Task security Nursing and physician leadership	Unit cohesiveness Managerial practices and staff response: **Communication** Coordination Problem-solving/conflict management	n/a

Non-hospital					
Haward et al. (2003)	Self-reported effectiveness: 31 measures across eight effectiveness groupings (e.g., within-team communication)	61 multi-disciplinary teams at primary care units	Team climate inventory Shared leadership of clinical decision making *Support for innovation*	Task characteristics Clarity of leadership	Team composition characteristics Discipline: proportion of breast care nurses
Bower, Campbell, Bojke, and Sibbald (2003)	Teams' self-reported ratings of effectiveness on professional practice, team working, patient-centered care, overall effectiveness, and team innovation	42 multi-disciplinary teams at primary care practices	Team climate subscales	n/a	**Length of employment** **Skill mix (clinician ratios)** Partnership status
Temkin-Greener et al. (2004)	Team effectiveness and performance	26 programs of all-inclusive care for the elderly (long-term geriatric care)	Adequacy of perceived resources Workplace conditions Leadership	**Communication** Coordination Conflict management Team cohesion	Personal and team characteristics: **Professional tenure** **Age** **Age diversity**
Poulton and West (1999)	Self-rated team effectiveness: organizational efficiency, teamwork, patient centered care, overall effectiveness	68 primary health teams at primary care units	*Emphasis on quality improvement* *Support for innovation*	**Clarity of goals, objectives and tasks** **Commitment to team objectives** Participation Health care practice	Team composition: Size **Tenure** Budget holding status

QI = quality improvement.
Italics: Athena survey indirectly captures this concept.
Bold: Athena survey explicitly measures this concept.

Hypothesis 1a. Group and developmental culture will be positively associated with perceived team effectiveness.

Hypothesis 1b. Hierarchical culture will be negatively associated with perceived team effectiveness.

Hypothesis 1c. An environment that supports collaboration will be positively associated with perceived team effectiveness.

Some individual and team (e.g., size, professional diversity) characteristics have also been found to predict team effectiveness. For example, working together longer should foster trust among team members. Status differences arising from differences in age, sex, or type of profession can influence the functioning of teams composed of members from many disciplines via levels of participation and influence (Bloom, 1980; Lichtenstein, Alexander, McCarthy, & Wells, 2004).

Hypothesis 2. Perceived team effectiveness will be higher among team members with longer professional tenure and higher status.

While each network will have its own unique measures of effectiveness, there are propositions regarding general determinants of network effectiveness. For example, based on various studies of mental health care providers, Provan and Milward (1995) have found that network effectiveness is highest under conditions of general network stability, especially when a network is centrally controlled and resources are adequate. Assuming networks become more stable over time, we develop the following hypotheses:

Hypothesis 3a. Perceived effectiveness at the team level will increase over time with membership in the network.

Hypothesis 3b. Team effectiveness will be positively associated with perceived network effectiveness.

DESIGN AND METHODS

Study Setting and Participants

The inter-organizational network of interest is the University of California (UC) Athena Breast Health Network, an innovative system of providing integrated breast care across the continuum from risk-based screening through survivorship care (Elson et al., 2013). The Athena Network is a hybrid collaborative project that creates a learning system incorporating both clinical care and research. Initiated in 2009 with funding from the Safeway Foundation and the UC Office of the President, the Network consists of five UC cancer centers and health systems (San Francisco, Irvine, San Diego, Los Angeles, and Davis) and a centralized management office. Its purpose is to drive patient-centered breast care including personalized prevention, screening, treatment, and survivorship. In the realm of screening, the goal was to recruit a cohort of 150,000 women receiving care at these cancer centers and health systems. Athena's other broad goal – carrying out collaborative cross-site clinical research integrated with clinical care – supports clinical care improvement through tailored screening and care to meet patient needs.

The Athena Network is a combination of multi-disciplinary teams within each site and is composed of focused working groups across sites. At each site a principal investigator, project manager, and breast health specialist are present, but the presence and involvement of other types of team members differ. Variations include the number and types of dedicated Athena staff (e.g., oncologist, primary care physician, radiologist, and patient navigator) and non-Athena staff (e.g., administrative, clinical, and volunteer), which may include people who work in other departments and support Athena by providing clinical services such as laboratory tests or information technology (IT) support. Variation in the degree the breast cancer team at each UC site is integrated into the site health system overall and within the business process of each of the respective departmental units also varies by UC site. Working groups and committees are also formed across UC sites, formally organized by breast care topic or discipline, as well as informally, usually organized by task or discipline.

The authors worked closely with site coordinators to generate the final list of invited participants, which included health professionals, program managers, support staff, and administrators closely and actively involved in Athena.

Data Collection

The data for the present study were collected via a self-administered *Qualtrics* survey over a two and a half year period. Subsequent to gaining approval by the UC Berkeley Institutional Review Board (IRB), the

Baseline survey was fielded in July 2010. To reduce respondent burden, several questionnaire items were removed[1] prior to Wave 2, which was fielded in December 2011, and Wave 3 in November 2012. At each of the three Waves, the sampling frame was finalized and participants were invited to complete the survey by email. Per IRB protocol, opt-out was available at all stages, as well as the option to take the survey over multiple time periods. Participants who had not yet opened the survey or who had unfinished surveys were sent email reminders every two weeks. At the close of the survey, partially completed questionnaires (the recipient started the survey but did not finish in the allotted time frame) were analyzed for the number of items completed.

Structured in-person interviews with purposively selected key informants (project managers, principal investigators, etc.) across the five medical centers were also conducted annually. During the Wave 3 interviews, we re-validated the content of the team effectiveness items by asking respondents to explain the score they had given on the survey (as was done for the Quality Improvement Implementation Survey, see Shortell et al., 1995).

Survey Measures: Dependent Variables

Perceived Network Effectiveness

Perceived network effectiveness was measured by participant agreement with the following statements: "Success in implementing elements of Athena will help: (1) improve the quality of care for patients with breast cancer; (2) improve patient satisfaction with care; (3) involve patients with their own care; (4) improve continuity of care; (5) you feel that you have accomplished something worthwhile; and (6) expand your Program's ability to secure research grants." Response options were (1) strongly disagree, (2) disagree, (3) agree and (4) strongly agree. As shown in Table 2, the six-item scale assessing these potentially positive impacts of successful implementation had high reliability ($\alpha = 0.93$ at Wave 3, 0.92 at Wave 2, 0.92 at Baseline).

Team Effectiveness

All respondents answered five questions regarding their cancer center as the "team": (1) how effective is the team at achieving its objectives?; (2) how effectively does the team operate "as a team"?; (3) how effectively does the team co-operate with other teams?; (4) how effectively does the team co-operate with the Center overall?; and (5) how effectively does the team

Table 2. Mean Scores, Internal Reliability, and Correlation with Team Effectiveness at Wave 3.

Variable/Scale	n	Mean	Range	S.D.	α	F	r
Team effectiveness	80	3.5		0.50	0.87	1.3	–
Information sources	85	2.8	1–4	0.65	0.83	2.0*	0.52***
Goals	80	2.8		0.49	0.77	1.5	0.69***
Communication	81	3.1		0.45	0.87	0.6	0.63***
Culture							
Group	75	26.4	0–100	16.8	0.80	1.7	0.51***
Developmental	75	22.9		12.4	0.73	1.8	0.06
Hierarchical	75	23.5		19.0	0.84	2.5**	−0.33***
Rational	75	27.2		13.0	0.70	1.7	−0.18
Supportive environment							
Colleague	77	1.5	1–3[a]	0.37	0.70	1.2	−0.40***
Authority	73	1.5		0.41	0.78	2.0*	−0.33**
Network effectiveness							
Potential impact of Athena	82	3.2	1–4	0.58	0.93	2.3*	0.34***

***$p<0.01$, **$p<0.05$, *$p<0.10$.

SD = standard deviation; α = Cronbach's alpha; F = test statistic from ANOVA for site; r = Spearman's rho.

[a]Lower score is more positive.

work to achieve the Athena Network goals? Scores for each item were an average of the responses on a four-point Likert scale indicating (1) not at all, (2) a little, (3) somewhat, and (4) very. Respondents who indicated that they belonged to a cross-site Athena working group or professional group (e.g., primary care providers) had the option of answering the same set of questions for their primary working group.

An overall team effectiveness scale constructed by averaging all five items had a Cronbach's alpha of 0.87 at Wave 3, compared to 0.91 at Wave 2 and 0.88 at Baseline. The team effectiveness items, as well as the information sources, goals, communication items described below, were adapted from the Quality Improvement Implementation Survey (Shortell et al., 1995). This instrument has been previously assessed for reliability in several health care team settings, including the Western Network Quality Improvement Study ($n=61$ hospitals) and in an evaluation of the Improving Chronic Illness Care Program ($n=40$ teams, see Shortell et al., 2004). Regarding content validity, key informants indicated that they understood effectiveness to mean getting tasks accomplished and successfully meeting goals.

Survey Measures: Independent Variables

Team Information Sources, Goals, and Communication

The same procedure was used to construct three other team-level variables, with Likert response options of: (1) strongly disagree, (2) disagree, (3) agree, and (4) strongly agree. The team information sources score ($\alpha = 0.83$ at Wave 3, 0.67 at Wave 2, 0.82 at Baseline) was an average of two items: (1) all team members are aware of where to go for information when they need it; and (2) it is not always obvious where we should go for information when we need it (reverse coded). Key informants understood this measure as knowing the contact person for information on specific Athena-related tasks including protocols and documents.

Content validity was less established for goals; during the validity check, some informants expressed uncertainty over what the Athena goals were, and there was little agreement on the distinction between group goals and Athena-wide goals. The team goals score ($\alpha = 0.77$ at Wave 3, 0.79 at Wave 2, 0.83 at Baseline) averaged four items: (1) all team members are clear about the overall goals of the team; (2) I hold the same opinion as other team members about how well the team is performing; (3) the team is clear about how it contributes to the overall Center goals; and (4) team members have different opinions about what the team should be trying to achieve (reverse coded).

Finally, a six-item team communication score ($\alpha = 0.87$ at Wave 3 and Wave 2, 0.89 at Baseline) averaged responses on: (1) team members act upon the information I communicate to them; (2) I am able to communicate effectively with team members; (3) this team has agreed upon methods for communication; (4) I regularly communicate with other members of the team; (5) communication between team members is unclear (reverse coded); and (6) I act upon the information that other members of the team communicate to me. The communication items were understood to indicate a lack of communication gaps.

Organizational Culture

The survey uses the competing values framework, in which respondents distribute 100 points across sets of organizational statements according to the descriptions that best fit their own organization (Zammuto & Krakower, 1991). The 100 points were distributed among four medical centers A through D emphasizing different values for each of the five sets of questions (medical center character, managers, cohesion, emphases, and rewards). Following the instructions of Quinn and Kimberly (1984), a score was computed for each of the four culture types for each respondent. Medical center level scores were then computed using the mean value of the individual scores for a specific culture type: group, developmental, rational, or hierarchical. This section of the survey was adapted from the Hospital Culture Instrument. This instrument has been previously validated in the health care team settings described above, as well as in the Health Systems Integration Study ($n = 11$ regions, see Shortell, Gillies, Anderson, Erickson, & Mitchell, 1996).

Support for Collaboration

Network members were asked to indicate the most likely response if they or any of their colleagues took any of five Athena-related actions: (1) would usually bring reward or approval, (2) would bring neither approval nor disapproval, (3) would usually bring admonition or disapproval, or (4) would not be noticed. The respondent considered the response to each action by a colleague and by someone in authority: (1) helping others implement elements of the Athena vision; (2) failing to follow new Athena policies and procedures (reverse coded); (3) suggesting new ways to implement elements of Athena; (4) failing to make efforts towards Athena vision implementation (reverse coded); and (5) collaborating with members of the Athena Network outside of one's own center. To approximate the existence of a supportive environment, an ordinal scale from 1 to 3 was created for answers of reward/approval, neither, and admonition/disapproval, with a lower mean indicating more support (see Table 2).

Individual Characteristics

Information on age, sex, years worked in profession and at one's cancer center, whether the respondent is a physician, and how much time the respondent spends on administrative tasks was collected. Participants also indicated their cancer center and membership in working groups.

Data Analysis

Univariate analyses are presented for all relevant variables as proportions or means. Bivariate analyses including chi-square tests, *t*-tests comparing overall to sub-group means, analysis of variance and correlations were used to test our hypotheses related to team effectiveness and other concepts at the individual and team levels. All scales were tested for internal reliability using data from each time period. All statistical analyses were carried out using STATA 13.0. To assess whether the items in our scales measured the same latent construct, we used Cronbach's alpha. As shown in Table 2, the reliability coefficients for scales that we hoped were measuring the same latent construct range from sufficient (0.70) to high (0.93). Finally, we analyzed results of within and between analyses from ANOVA to test whether variation between each of the five medical centers was greater than variation within each center (Charns et al., 2012; Valentine et al., 2011).

RESULTS

Sample

The response rate was 47% at Baseline ($n=75$), 68% at Wave 2 ($n=108$), and 69% at Wave 3 ($n=86$).[2] Partially completed surveys were retained if participants had completed at least 15% of the survey (when meaningful responses began to be recorded). Of the 124 eligible Wave 3 participants, 2 opted out, 5 did not complete enough items to be included, and the sessions of the remaining 31 people expired (the recipient never started the survey). Site-specific response rates are reported in Table 4. Of the 158 eligible Wave 2 participants, 2 opted out and 48 sessions expired.

The three Waves were treated as independent samples, though there was respondent overlap. All observations were de-identified once data were exported from *Qualtrics*, but a comparison of the Wave 2 and 3 completed sampling lists indicates that 49 Wave 3 responders (57%) had completed a survey at Wave 2; 45% of those who were surveyed at Wave 2 went on to complete a survey at Wave 3.

Compared with previous years, Wave 3 respondents were younger, more likely to be female, and less likely to be a physician (Table 3). A significantly larger proportion participated in more than one working group: 81% participate in more than one working group, compared with 65% one year ago and 44% two years ago. More than three quarters of respondents were women and 17% were under the age of 30 – more than double the proportion at baseline. Since the sample is younger than previous years, mean professional tenure has decreased by about 1.5 years since Baseline. The proportion of respondents employed for more than five years at their current center (18%) has decreased steadily and significantly from Baseline (59%) and Wave 2 (39%) (Fig. 2).

Table 3. Demographics at Baseline, Wave 2, and Wave 3.

Respondent Characteristic	Baseline	*n*	Wave 2	*n*	Wave 3	*n*
Total number of respondents	75	–	108	–	86	–
Female	65%	45	70%	76	77%	66
Over 50 years old	46%	31	46%	37	43%	32
Under 30 years old	7%	5	9%	7	17%*	13
Physician	42%	29	41%	33	35%	29
Senior Executive	24%	18	15%	16	17%	15
Dedicates >33% of time to admin. tasks	32%	22	25%	20	40%	30
Worked at current center >5 years	59%	41	38%**	31	18%***	14
Worked at current center ≤ 5 years	41%	28	62%**	50	82%***	64
Mean number of years in profession	17.4	64	17.6	74	16	75
Part of more than one working group	44%	33	65%**	70	81%***	68

***$p < 0.001$, **$p < 0.01$, *$p < 0.10$.

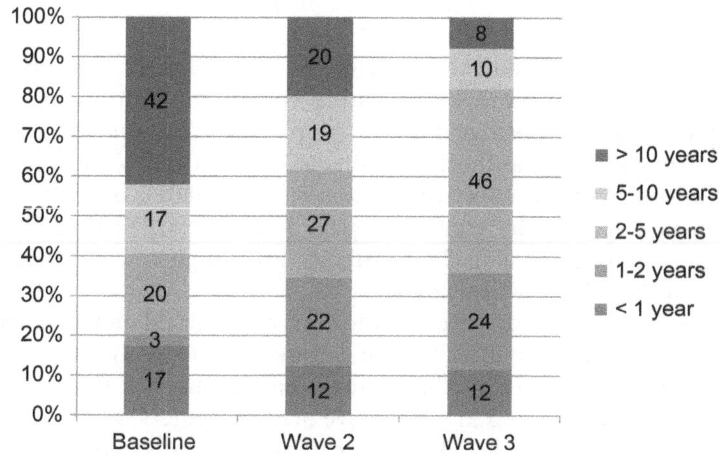

Fig. 2. Years Worked at Current Center at Baseline ($n = 69$), Wave 2 ($n = 81$), and Wave 3 ($n = 78$).

Table 4 displays demographic characteristics for each site at Wave 3. There was substantial variation by site, but few statistically significant differences. Compared to the other medical centers, nearly a third (30%) of respondents reported working at their current center for more than five years at Site 5 ($p = 0.03$).

Table 4. Demographics for Individual Medical Centers, Wave 3.

Respondent Characteristic	Site 1	Site 2	Site 3	Site 4	Site 5
Female	57%*	85%	67%	76%	83%
Over 50 years old	46%	62%	33%	33%	50%
Under 30 years old	15%	8%	22%	7%	20%
Physician	43%	46%	33%	35%	30%
Executive Committee member	21%	23%	17%	12%	17%
Dedicates >33% of time to admin. Tasks	33%	31%	40%	20%*	50%
Worked at current center >5 years	14%	15%	0%	17%	30%**
Mean number years in profession	20.2	19.2	11.5	14.2	15.8
Part of more than one working group	77%	83%	67%	82%	83%
Total number of respondents	14	13	12	17	23
Response rate	78%	59%	52%	74%	77%

$^{**}p<0.05$, $^{*}p<0.10$.

Team-Level Findings

As measured by the F statistic reported in Table 2, there was more variation between medical centers than within centers for information sources, hierarchical culture, positive impact on patient care, and perception of support from those in authority at Wave 3. Based on Wave 2 responses, the F statistic for team effectiveness was 3.25 ($p=0.01$), indicating greater variation in responses by medical center. T-tests revealed that Site 1 had significantly lower and Site 2 had significantly higher team effectiveness scores than the other medical centers.

Besides the overall cross-site variation for hierarchical culture, there were clear distributional differences for the culture types (Fig. 3). Developmental culture scores were lowest at the medical centers that had the highest hierarchical scores (Sites 1 and 2). Of the five medical centers, rational culture is most prevalent at Sites 4 and 5 (more than 29 points), and significantly less so at Site 3 where it received only 20.8 points. Sites 3 and 5 scored significantly lower on Hierarchical culture (14 and 15.7 points, respectively), while the opposite trend was observed for Site 1 (35.2 points). Site 4 scored significantly lower (20.6) on Group culture than the other sites.

Partial support for Hypothesis 1a was found, as group (but not developmental) culture was significantly and positively associated with team effectiveness at all three time points (Table 5). Moreover, the correlation grew larger and more significant over time. Hypothesis 1b was partially supported when analyzed by survey year: the association between hierarchical culture and team effectiveness was always negative, but didn't gain

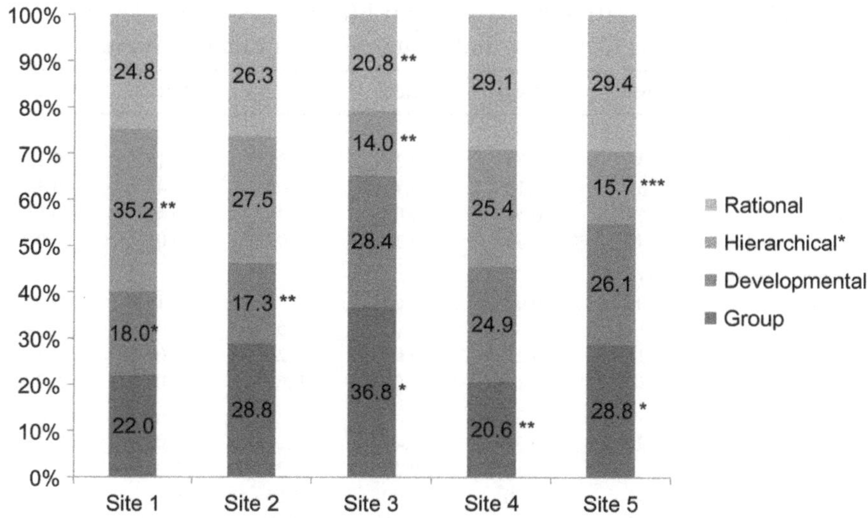

Fig. 3. Organizational Culture Distributions for Individual Medical Centers, Wave 3. $*p<0.10$, $**p<0.05$, $***p<0.01$.

Table 5. Correlation between Team Effectiveness and Organizational Culture at Baseline, Wave 2, and Wave 3.

Organizational Culture Type	Baseline	Wave 2	Wave 3
Rational	−0.07	−0.27*	−0.18
Hierarchical	−0.10	−0.18	−0.33**
Group	0.26*	0.39***	0.51***
Developmental	0.01	0.15	0.06

$***p<0.001$, $**p<0.01$, $*p<0.05$.

significance until Wave 3. Given the site-specific variation in culture types, we examined correlations by individual medical center (Table 6). The group and hierarchical culture pattern was strongest at Sites 1 and 5 at Wave 3.

With a lower value indicating more support, respondents felt most support for the perceived reaction to helping others implement elements of the Athena vision at Wave 3 (mean of 1.3, Table 7). Since Baseline, scores have tended to slightly decrease (although not significantly so) indicating more support for Athena-related actions over the years. Participants did not differentiate substantially between likely colleague and authority responses to actions; the overall scales were highly correlated ($r=0.63$, $p<0.001$).

Table 6. Correlation between Team Effectiveness Variables and Organizational Culture at Individual Medical Centers, Wave 3.

Variable	Site 1	Site 2	Site 3	Site 4	Site 5	All
Team effectiveness						
Rational	−0.48	−0.37	0.30	−0.25	0.18	−0.18
Hierarchical	−0.67**	−0.10	0.10	0.01	−0.48**	−0.33***
Group	0.68**	0.54*	0.09	0.26	0.47**	0.51***
Developmental	0.47	−0.44	−0.30	−0.07	−0.05	0.06
Team information sources						
Rational	0.03	−0.02	−0.02	0.05	0.14	0.04
Hierarchical	0.14	−0.36	0.05	−0.56**	−0.07	−0.24**
Group	−0.14	0.22	−0.09	0.20	0.02	0.18
Developmental	−0.15	0.16	0.02	0.61**	0.03	0.22**
Team goals						
Rational	−0.21	−0.35	0.47	−0.51*	0.08	−0.11
Hierarchical	−0.47	−0.19	0.20	−0.24	−0.28	−0.37***
Group	0.45	0.50*	−0.005	0.55**	0.13	0.47***
Developmental	0.37	−0.18	−0.36	0.29	0.11	0.18
Team communication						
Rational	−0.24	−0.29	0.52	−0.07	0.05	−0.005
Hierarchical	−0.68**	−0.32	−0.37	−0.09	−0.16	−0.29**
Group	0.52*	0.62**	−0.09	0.02	−0.02	0.32***
Developmental	0.61**	−0.24	0.04	0.21	0.12	0.15

***$p<0.01$, **$p<0.05$, *$p<0.10$.

As shown in Table 2, hypothesis 1c was supported by the significant correlation between the supportive environment scales and team effectiveness. This finding has been consistent since Wave 2 ($r=-0.40$ for colleague, $p<0.001$; $r=-0.26$ for authority, $p=0.04$) and Baseline ($r=-0.37$ for colleague, $p<0.003$).

Individual Level Findings

On a scale of 1–4, the overall mean team effectiveness score for the entire sample was 3.5, with a standard deviation of 0.5 at Wave 3 (Table 2). Hypothesis 2 was not supported, as there were no statistically significant differences on the overall team effectiveness score by respondent characteristics at either Wave 3 or Baseline (data not shown). At Wave 2, physicians scored team effectiveness significantly lower than non-physicians (3.1 versus 3.4, $p=0.03$), as did respondents who had worked more than five years at their center.

Table 7. Supportive Environment Score[a] at Baseline, Wave 2, and Wave 3.

Response to Athena-related Action	Baseline		Wave 2		Wave 3	
	Mean (S.D.)	*n*	Mean (S.D.)	*n*	Mean (S.D.)	*n*
Helping others implement elements of Athena vision						
A colleague	1.4 (0.53)	64	1.4 (0.51)	85	1.3 (0.48)	73
Those in authority	n/a	–	1.4 (0.52)	74	1.3 (0.47)	69
Failing to follow new Athena policies and procedures[b]						
A colleague	1.6 (0.55)	58	2.2 (0.75)	84	1.5 (0.56)	62
Those in authority	n/a	–	2.1 (0.74)	78	1.5 (0.62)	63
Suggesting new ways to implement elements of Athena						
A colleague	1.5 (0.53)	66	1.4 (0.54)	85	1.4 (0.50)	72
Those in authority	n/a	–	1.4 (0.58)	72	1.4 (0.50)	67
Failing to make efforts towards Athena vision implementation[b]						
A colleague	1.5 (0.57)	56	2.4 (0.72)	85	1.6 (0.56)	60
Those in authority	n/a	–	2.3 (0.75)	80	1.6 (0.64)	60
Collaborating with network members outside center						
By a colleague	1.4 (0.48)	62	1.5 (0.57)	80	1.4 (0.53)	62
Those in authority	n/a	–	1.5 (0.58)	69	1.3 (0.50)	63
Colleague scale	1.5 (0.32)	69	1.5 (0.36)	88	1.5 (0.37)	77
Authority scale	n/a	–	1.5 (0.40)	77	1.5 (0.41)	73

[a]A lower score means more likely to reward and less likely to admonish.
[b]Item reverse coded to calculate overall mean score.

Network Level Findings

In support of Hypothesis 3a, overall team effectiveness scores have increased significantly over time (from 3.0, to 3.3, to 3.5, $p<0.001$, data not shown) and are consistently rated higher than the information sources, goals, and communication scores, which have increased slightly or remained the same since Baseline. As shown in Table 8, Hypothesis 3b was also supported. Our network effectiveness indicator was positively and significantly correlated with team effectiveness at all three time points, despite variation between sites.

LIMITATIONS

While our response rate compares favorably with similar studies based on surveys of health professionals (e.g., Greene, Hart, & Wagner, 2005; Poulton & West, 1999; Temkin-Greener et al., 2004), we cannot rule out

Table 8. Mean Perceived Network Effectiveness and Correlation with Team Effectiveness at Individual Medical Centers at Baseline, Wave 2, and Wave 3.

Network Effectiveness	Baseline		Wave 2		Wave 3	
	Mean (S.D.)	*r*	Mean (S.D.)	*r*	Mean (S.D.)	*r*
Overall	3.2 (0.52)	0.34**	3.2 (0.56)	0.42***	3.2 (0.58)	0.34**
Site 1	3.2 (0.47)	0.55	3.1 (0.47)	0.77**	3.2 (0.66)	0.27
Site 2	3.5 (0.44)	0.42	3.1 (0.73)	0.56*	3.2 (0.42)	0.19
Site 3	2.9 (0.54)	0.40	3.0 (0.52)	0.59	3.1 (0.56)	0.72**
Site 4	3.2 (0.56)	−0.10	3.1 (0.38)*	−0.15	3.1 (0.51)	0.18
Site 5	3.3 (0.43)	0.46	3.5 (0.39)	0.43	3.5 (0.44)	0.64**

***$p<0.001$, **$p<0.01$, *$p<0.05$.

selection bias given the optional nature of the survey. Despite assuring participants that their responses would be kept confidential, self-report data could also have resulted in a positive bias, but would likely be consistent across sites and over time. The study, of course, examines correlations only and therefore, cannot conclude that a certain type of culture "causes" team effectiveness or that team effectiveness, in turn, "causes" greater satisfaction or perceptions of progress over time.

DISCUSSION

Teams operating in an inter-organizational context have dual challenges and goals: (1) to continue to function effectively to achieve the goals and objectives of their own individual organizations (in our study, each Athena site) and (2) to concurrently promote and achieve the goals and objectives of the network. At times, these goals and objectives may be in conflict or at the very least create an ongoing tension in terms of allocation of time, resources, and priorities. Factors particular to each site which may also affect the network include differential use of electronic medical record platforms, the organization of cancer care models (i.e., the medical center has a dedicated breast care center vs. a general cancer center), physical and geographical placement of teams, funding arrangements, and access to non-Athena resources (e.g., phlebotomy services). Addressing these issues requires longitudinal data that can assess how teams evolve to navigate and meet their dual commitments.

Our findings suggest that ongoing interaction over time serves to develop the shared goals, norms, knowledge, and respect required for effective inter-organizational collaboration, along with identification of the comparative advantage of each organizational member to the network. We found support for our hypotheses regarding greater team effectiveness over time and a positive association with greater perceived network effectiveness. These findings corroborate qualitative data showing that key informant ratings of Athena's progress were higher at Wave 3 than Wave 2 for every site.

Findings suggest that team processes are also important to inter-organizational effectiveness. "Organizational design affects performance through its effects on coordination networks" within and between organizations, and this type of coordination is based on inter-personal relations or "relational coordination" (Gittell & Weiss, 2004, p. 141). In other words, people form relationships via meetings, phone calls, and cross-site working groups, which impact care improvement processes because trust and understanding of roles are gained, leading to better coordination.

IMPLICATIONS FOR RESEARCH AND PRACTICE

Being part of an inter-organizational network provides individual teams with an outside peer group or benchmark reference group against which they can measure themselves in order to improve; to pull their own weight so as not to be perceived as "free rider" and, positively, to impress or "look good" to their peers. This mechanism would also support our findings linking team effectiveness to our indicator of network effectiveness, the perceived potential impact of Athena on patient care. The perception of ability to meet patient needs is associated with team effectiveness (Temkin-Greener et al., 2004); future research could further explore how inter-organizational network activities influence patient needs and vice-versa.

The fact that culture distribution scores varied significantly among cancer centers supports its use as a team-level construct. The positive correlations between group culture and team effectiveness, goals, and communication were largely driven by two to three medical centers, while the relationship between information sources and culture was highly influenced by one medical center. Future studies should use multilevel regression modeling to simultaneously examine the relationships between culture, team effectiveness, and other variables at the different levels of analysis: self, team (own center), and the overall network, across the three years.

Since organizational culture appears to be consistently associated with team performance, health care managers, and organizations that focus on values associated with group affiliation, teamwork and participation, and risk-taking, innovation and change may have a greater impact on patient care. Research is now needed on examining the relationship between these cultural values and the actual attainment of the network goal and objectives.

As the health care sector continues to undergo significant organizational transformation such as further development of integrated health care systems, accountable care organizations, and networks of medical homes, there is a need to understand the mechanisms such as the use of inter-professional and multi-disciplinary teams that contribute to success or failure. Further research building on this exploratory study of five health systems is needed to examine such factors as the role of payment incentives, internal reward systems, the use of electronic health records, public disclosure of performance data, and depth of leadership within each organization and within the network overall in influencing team effectiveness, and subsequently network performance.

NOTES

1. The following items were removed after Baseline: 15 items assessing the benefits and costs of participation in Athena, 3 items regarding potential effects of adopting and implementing the Athena model, 12 items assessing the importance of elements of Athena professionally and at one's Center, 11 items on coordination with and between cancer centers, and 15 items related to perceived team effectiveness. Four items on coordination with and between cancer centers were removed after Wave 2.

2. Due to concerns about anonymity, the Baseline sampling list was not stored for future use. The survey platform also changed between Baseline and Wave 2. Since individual Baseline participants cannot be identified, the response rate was calculated based on the Wave 2 sampling list; it may be underestimated.

ACKNOWLEDGEMENTS

We are grateful to members of the Athena Breast Health Network for their participation in this study. We are also thankful for the funding support from the Safeway Foundation and the University of California Office of the President which made this study possible.

REFERENCES

Bloom, J. R. (1980). Status characteristics, leadership consensus and decision-making among nurses. *Social Science and Medicine, 14A*, 15–22.

Bower, P., Campbell, S., Bojke, C., & Sibbald, B. (2003). Team structure, team climate and the quality of care in primary care: An observational study. *Quality and Safety in Health Care, 12*, 273–279.

Charns, M. P., Foster, M. K., Alligood, E. C., Benzer, J. K., Burgess, J. F., Li, D., ... Clauser, S. B. (2012). Multilevel interventions: Measurement and measures. *Journal of the National Cancer Institute Monographs, 44*, 67–77.

Cohen, S. G., & Bailey, D. R. (1997). What makes teams work: Group effectiveness research from the shop floor to the executive suite. *Journal of Management, 23*(4), 238–290.

Cretin, S., Shortell, S., & Keeler, E. B. (2004). An evaluation of collaborative interventions to improve chronic illness care: Framework and study design. *Evaluation Review, 28*, 28–51.

Edmonson, A. (1999). Psychological safety and learning behavior in work teams. *Administrative Science Quarterly, 44*, 350–383.

Elson, S. L., Hiatt, R. A., Anton-Culver, H., Howell, L. P., Naeim, A., Parker, B. A., & Esserman, L. J. (2013). The Athena breast health network: Developing a rapid learning system in breast cancer prevention, screening, treatment, and care. *Breast Cancer Research and Treatment, 140*(2), 417–425.

Gittell, J. H., & Weiss, L. (2004). Coordination networks within and across organizations: A multi-level framework. *Journal of Management Studies, 41*(1), 127–153.

Greene, S. M., Hart, G., & Wagner, E. H. (2005). Measuring and improving performance in multicenter research consortia. *Journal of the National Cancer Institute Monographs, 35*, 26–32.

Hagen, N. A., Stiles, C. R., Biondo, P. D., Cummings, G. G., Fainsinger, R. L., Moulin, D. E. ... Spice, R. (2011). Establishing a multicentre clinical research network: Lessons learned. *Current Oncology, 18*(5), e243–e249.

Haward, R., Amir, Z., Borill, C., Dawson, J., Scully, J., West, M., & Sainsbury, R. (2003). Breast cancer teams: The impact of constitution, new cancer workload, and methods of operation on effectiveness. *British Journal of Cancer, 89*, 15–22.

Health Care Delivery System Reform and The Patient Protection & Affordable Care Act. (2012, March). *A Report from Senator Sheldon Whitehouse for the U.S. Senate Committee on Health, Education, Labor & Pensions*. Retrieved from: http://www.whitehouse.senate.gov/download/?id=a8ae94dc-d490-47a1-bd61-a11c5f161613&download=1

Howard, M., Brazil, K., Akhtar-Danesh, N., & Agarwal, G. (2011). Self-reported teamwork in family health team practices in Ontario: Organizational and cultural predictors of team climate. *Canadian Family Physician, 57*, e185–e191.

Lemieux-Charles, L., & McGuire, W. L. (2006). What do we know about health care team effectiveness? A review of the literature. *Medical Care Research and Review, 63*, 263–300.

Lemieux-Charles, L., Murray, M., Baker, G. R., Barnsley, J., Tasa, K., & Ibrahim, S. A. (2002). The effects of quality improvement practices on team effectiveness: A mediational model. *Journal of Organizational Behavior, 23*, 533–553.

Lichtenstein, R., Alexander, J. A., McCarthy, J. F., & Wells, R. (2004). Status differences in cross-functional teams: Effects on individual member participation, job satisfaction and intent to quit. *Journal of Health and Social Behavior, 45*(3), 322–333.

Nembhard, I. M., Singer, S. J., Shortell, S. M., Rittenhouse, D., & Casalino, L. P. (2012). The cultural complexity of medical groups. *Health Care Management Review*, *37*(3), 200–213.

Poulton, B. C., & West, M. A. (1999). The determinants of effectiveness in primary health care teams. *Journal of Interprofessional Care*, *13*(1), 7–18.

Powell, W. W. (1987). Hybrid organizational arrangements: New form or transitional development? *California Management Review*, *30*, 67–87.

Provan, K. G., & Milward, H. B. (1995). A preliminary theory of inter-organizational network effectiveness: A study of four community mental health systems. *Administrative Science Quarterly*, *40*, 1–33.

Quinn, R. E., & Kimberly, J. R. (1984). Paradox, planning, and perseverance: Guidelines for managerial practice. In J. R. Kimberly & R. E. Quinn (Eds.), *Managing organization transitions* (pp. 295–313). Homewood, IL: Dow Jones-Irwin.

Scott, W. R. (2003). Chapter 8: Boundary setting and boundary spanning. In W. R. Scott (Ed.), *Organizations: Rational, natural and open systems* (5th ed., pp. 185–229). Homewood, IL: Dow Jones-Irwin.

Shortell, S. M., Gillies, R. R., Anderson, D. A., Erickson, K. M., & Mitchell, J. B. (1996). *Remaking health care in America: Building organized delivery systems*. Upper Saddle River, NJ: Prentice Hall.

Shortell, S. M., Marsteller, J. A., Lin, M., Pearson, M. L., Wu, S. Y., Mendel, P. ... Rosen, M. (2004). The role of perceived team effectiveness in improving chronic illness care. *Medical Care*, *42*(11), 1040–1048.

Shortell, S. M., O'Brien, J. L., Carman, J. M., Foster, R. W., Hughes, E. F., Boerstler, H., & O'Connor, E. J. (1995). Assessing the impact of continuous quality improvement/total quality management: Concept versus implementation. *Health Services Research*, *30*(2), 377–401.

Shortell, S. M., Rousseau, D. M., Gillies, R. R., Devers, K. J., & Simons, T. L. (1991). Organizational assessment in intensive care units (ICUs): Construct development, reliability and validity of the ICU nurse-physician questionnaire. *Medical Care*, *29*(8), 709–726.

Temkin-Greener, H., Gross, D., Kunitz, S. J., & Mukamel, D. (2004). Measuring interdisciplinary team performance in a long-term care setting. *Medical Care*, *42*(5), 472–480.

Valentine, M. A., Nembhard, I. M., & Edmondson, A. C. (2011, September). *Measuring teamwork in health care settings: A review of survey instruments*. Working Paper No. 11-116. Harvard Business School, Boston, MA.

Vinokur-Kaplan, D. (1995). Treatment teams that work (and those that don't): An application of Hackman's group effectiveness model to interdisciplinary teams in psychiatric hospitals. *Journal of Applied Behavioural Science*, *31*(3), 303–327.

Zammuto, R., & Krakower, J. (1991). Quantitative and qualitative studies of organizational culture. In R. W. Woodman & W. A. Pasmore (Eds.), *Research in organizational change and development* (pp. 83–114). Greenwich, CT: JAI Press.

A BUSINESS PLANNING MODEL TO IDENTIFY NEW SAFETY NET CLINIC LOCATIONS

James Langabeer, II, Jeffrey Helton, Jami DelliFraine, Ebbin Dotson, Carolyn Watts and Karen Love

ABSTRACT

Purpose – *Community health clinics serving the poor and underserved are geographically expanding due to changes in U.S. health care policy. This paper describes the experience of a collaborative alliance of health care providers in a large metropolitan area who develop a conceptual and mathematical decision model to guide decisions on expanding its network of community health clinics.*

Design/methodology/approach – *Community stakeholders participated in a collaborative process that defined constructs they deemed important in guiding decisions on the location of community health clinics. This collaboration also defined key variables within each construct. Scores for variables within each construct were then totaled and weighted into a community-specific optimal space planning equation. This analysis relied entirely on secondary data available from published sources.*

Population Health Management in Health Care Organizations
Advances in Health Care Management, Volume 16, 95–112

ISSN: 1474-8231/doi:10.1108/S1474-823120140000016005

Findings – *The model built from this collaboration revolved around the constructs of demand, sustainability, and competition. It used publicly available data defining variables within each construct to arrive at an optimal location that maximized demand and sustainability and minimized competition.*

Practical implications – *This is a model that safety net clinic planners and community stakeholders can use to analyze demographic and utilization data to optimize capacity expansion to serve uninsured and Medicaid populations.*

Originality/value – *Communities can use this innovative model to develop a locally relevant clinic location-planning framework.*

Keywords: Community health planning; community health centers; medically uninsured; community health services

Recent federal policy changes in the United States create important new opportunities as well as challenges for community health centers (CHCs) that serve the poor, under-insured, and uninsured. These health centers, including privately funded charity clinics and federally qualified health centers (FQHCs), provide a critical resource for their target population. The American Recovery and Reinvestment Act and the Patient Protection and Affordable Care Act (collectively "ACA" hereafter) together make significant reforms that both directly and indirectly affect the sustainability of CHCs. As a result, CHCs have critical decisions to make regarding services provided, capacity, and capital financing. However, their decision-making processes are complicated by the complex external environment created by their diverse funding sources, charitable purpose, and (for FQHCs) their quasi-public status and need to comply with state and federal regulations and requirements. Thus, CHCs must have a decision model that balances the competing demands of the stakeholders in this external environment, including donors, volunteers, governments, patients, and citizens, without losing sight of internal organizational needs.

This paper shares the experience of one Texas community in developing a flexible heuristic-based CHC decision model. Because an important impact of the ACA is on grant funding for CHC capacity, we will focus specifically on expansion and location decisions. We will begin with a description of CHCs, their target population, and their funding sources.

We will then describe existing public policy that affects CHC operations and decision making, and the impact of the ACA. We will outline the decision-making model developed in Houston and conclude with some observations about the impact of the uncertainties surrounding the implementation of the ACA on CHC sustainability.

BACKGROUND

In 2010, there were 1,124 federally funded FQHCs in 8,100 locations in every state in the United States, plus Washington, DC, and all US territories (Kaiser Family Foundation, 2012). These health centers achieve their federally qualified status by meeting four conditions:

1. Location in or service to medically underserved communities (as defined by the federal government)
2. Provision of comprehensive primary care services in accordance with federal guidelines
3. Prospective adjustment of charges based on patients' ability to pay
4. Governance by a board of directors, the majority of whose members are patients of the health center

FQHCs receive direct grant funding from the federal government under Section 330 of the Public Health Service Act (PHS Act Section 330). In addition, these centers receive special payment for services provided to public patients (Medicare and Medicaid) and have access to the benefits of other federal programs (Nat'l Assoc of CHCs).

There were also 100 "look-alike" FQHCs in 2010. These CHCs meet the above-mentioned four conditions and receive special payments but do not receive Section 330 grant funding. Finally, there are other CHCs that do not meet all the conditions required to be a FQHC or a look-alike but still serve the same target population. These CHCs receive no federal grants or special payments for public patients (Kaiser Family Foundation, 2012).

Funding for CHCs comes from Section 330 grants (for FQHCs only), state and federal payment for services provided to Medicaid and Medicare patients, charitable donations, and direct out-of-pocket payments for services by patients who can afford to pay. The Kaiser Foundation reports that 60% of the patients treated by CHCs are between the ages of 19 and 65, 70% have incomes below 100% of the federal poverty level (FPL), 36% are uninsured, and 49% live in rural areas (Nat'l Assoc of CHCs).

CHCs and Public Policy

A variety of local, state, and federal policies affect the operations of CHCs. Local zoning laws directly constrain location decisions. State licensing and scope of practice laws influence the breadth of the services provided and the clinicians who provide them. State and federal policy dictates payment for services provided to public patients as well the other conditions of FQHC and look-alike status. Indirectly, state and federal Medicaid policy has a large impact on CHCs by determining eligibility for the primary source of coverage for low-income individuals. Medicaid, as a shared state/federal program, allows states a great deal of flexibility in this determination. As a result, there is wide variability in the conditions of eligibility and the numbers of enrollees across states. In January 2013, income levels for eligibility among jobless parents of dependent children ranged from 10% FPL in Alabama to 215% FPL in Minnesota. Non-disabled childless adults were not covered at any income level in all but nine states. In 2013, Texas Medicaid covers jobless parents with incomes below 12% FPL and does not cover childless adults.

The ACA

President Obama signed the ACA into law in March 2010. In July 2012, the US Supreme Court upheld the controversial individual coverage mandate but rendered voluntary the provision that states expand Medicaid eligibility to all individuals with incomes at or below 138% FPL. There are many provisions in the 2000+ page statute that affect CHCs directly or indirectly, but there are several of most relevance to this paper. First and most directly, the ACA authorizes $11 billion in *new* funding for FQHC expansion ($9.5B) and capital projects ($1.5B). These funds are added to the existing Section 330 program. The goal is to increase the number of patients served by FQHCs by 20 million by 2015. Other clearly advantageous provisions require all health plans offered through the newly created public insurance exchanges to contract with FQHCs, and set minimum payment rates to FQHCs at no less than Medicaid prospective payment rates (Department of Health and Human Services, 2011; Hofer, Abraham, & Moscovice, 2011; National Association of Community Health Centers, 2013).

There are other provisions, however, that offer challenges as well as opportunities for CHCs. While the individual mandate means that more CHC patients may have insurance and/or may have better insurance because of the substantial subsidies available through the exchanges, CHCs may have to compete for them. There is little competition for patients who are unable to pay. However, that may not be true once they become insured. Further, since states are not required to expand Medicaid, 25 states (including Texas) are not moving forward with expansion at this time (Kaiser Family Foundation, 2012). Because the architects of the ACA intended for Medicaid expansion to be universal, they built in provisions based on that premise. Thus, individuals between existing eligibility income levels and the intended new Medicaid eligibility level (138% FPL) do not have access to subsidies through the exchanges. Further, special payments ("DSH" payments) made to hospitals that treat a disproportionate share of indigent patients will be significantly reduced over the next few years, jeopardizing the financial health of a crucial care partner of CHCs. As a result, safety net providers in non-expanding states such as Texas will have fewer resources from one source (DSH payments) with no offsetting revenue from other sources (Medicaid payments or insurance payments).

For individuals who are able to afford subsidized insurance through the exchanges, coverage will necessarily include a reasonably broad array of services, including behavioral health, prescription drugs, and certain preventive services.

Taken together, the policy changes put in place by the ACA create the need for careful decision making – including decisions about expansion and new clinic location – within CHCs.

PLANNING FRAMEWORK

Establishing an optimal location for a business is a fundamental component of strategic business planning. Demographic factors such as population, income, access to transportation, and proximity to competitors impact a business' viability and sustainability (Spaeder, 2010). Organizations must choose a location that will meet the needs of its customers (short- and long-term) and stay financially sustainable, even as demographic populations shift and environmental conditions change (Owen & Daskin, 1998). A new facility is a major investment for most organizations, one which requires significant expenditures of time and money. Choosing the wrong location for a new facility can result in wasted resources, and many organizations, especially non-profit health care organizations, already operate on thin profit margins.

Choosing an optimal location for a non-profit CHC involves more than simply choosing the most profitable location. Because CHCs focus on services to medically underserved populations (MUPs), the business model for the community clinic is different from that of a retail business or even a more traditional physician group practice clinic (Health Resources and Services Administration, 2010). Patients served by the CHC usually cannot pay for services and so these organizations receive designation as an FQHC (with preferential access to government funding) by proximity to areas that do not have adequate access to primary care services. These patients may have lower paying Medicaid insurance coverage not usually accepted by the traditional physician group practice that can build a preferable business case based on proximity to patient populations that have higher paying commercial insurance resources.

The mission and governance of different types CHCs influence how location decisions are made. Business planning decisions for the FQHC and FQHC look-alikes differ from privately funded charity clinics, which accept no government funding. Primary among these differences is identification of areas that are designated as a medically underserved area (MUA) or containing a MUP. MUPs are defined groups of people with a specified barrier to accessing medical care through "mainstream" providers, many of whom are unable to communicate in English or find a culturally sensitive provider. MUAs and MUPs are defined based on the analysis of local demographic data by HRSA. FQHC or FQHC look-alike clinics wishing to establish a new CHC would first need to identify where MUA or MUP locations exist, or try to obtain MUA or MUP designation for a new area. Privately funded charity clinics are not restricted to specific locations by government regulations. Those clinics serve a population that due to impoverishment, experience limited ability to travel to clinics to access care services. Thus, all three types of CHCs must consider their proximity to targeted underserved patient populations. Post-ACA, CHCs must also consider competition from existing providers and the availability of resources (both private and public health insurance, and private and public donations) to sustain a new clinic's operations.

Sustainability for a CHC depends heavily on access to insured patients with resources available to pay for care, beyond the core populations served by an FQHC or FQHC look-alike facility. To the extent that a new CHC could diversify its revenue streams to include privately insured patients, the long-term survival of the entity would be better assured, particularly should a major funding source such as FQHC funds or private grant donations be significantly reduced (Mims, 2006). Diversified revenue sources are specifically noted as a long-term survival strategy for safety net providers (Bovbjerg & Ullman, 2001), but the challenge for CHCs is how to best meet the needs of targeted underserved patient populations while still being easily accessible to patients with the ability to pay for services. While Medicaid funding levels are below those desired by physicians in traditional private clinic settings, those payments are desirable in a clinic setting where patients tend to be uninsured. Hence, proximity to patients with insurance – including Medicaid – supports sustainability of a CHC organization to a greater extent than that desirable in the private clinic setting.

CHCs also need to consider other sources of revenue including grants from local and city governments, private donors (individuals or foundations), endowments or trusts, civic, and/or religious organizations. Because they are a potential source of funding for CHCs, these organizations may also play a significant role in determining an optimal location for a new CHC. However, location-planning models described in the literature generally address only demand, distance, and travel time as inputs into a mathematical location decision model (Owen & Daskin, 1998). These decision models do not adequately consider all of the inputs into the CHC business model, including the needs, demands, influence of, and potential revenue from community stakeholders. Further, they do not consider the variables defining the unique niche served by the CHC – patients without health insurance or with Medicaid insurance paying at low levels. Thus, engaging community stakeholders in providing input into CHC facility planning could help ensure future financial sustainability. We describe the planning process for a new CHC in Houston, Texas that incorporates stakeholder input into a mathematical decision model.

METHODOLOGY

Clinic Location Planning Model Development

To provide health care services for the poor and underserved, communities would ideally establish a complex linkage of clinics, hospitals, and health systems. However, Houston's existing safety net suffers from high patient demand, low provider capacity, and uncertain organizational sustainability. The Harris County Healthcare Alliance ("Alliance") is a non-profit organization representing over 50 health care organizations in the Houston area.

The mission of the Alliance is to coordinate efforts among member organizations to help care for the uninsured and underserved in Harris County (http://www.hchalliance.org/member-area.html). Members include hospitals, health systems, and non-profit community groups that collaborate to address community health care problems. The Alliance, its financial supporters, community stakeholders, and local university researchers used a Delphi technique to create a conceptual planning decision-making model to select new locations for CHCs that would best serve the community. The group met three times over the course of three months to reach consensus.

There are nearly 100 community health care center sites operating in Harris County. Alliance members agreed that any new CHC facilities should address patient demand, have a minimal impact on existing providers, and maximize opportunities to diversify revenue streams. The Alliance discussed site selection model research focused on meeting customer demand by maximizing proximity to potential users of services. Among the earliest works in this area is that of Toregas, Swain, ReVelle, and Bergman (1971), which identified sites to provide emergency services in a given area. Organizational adaptability models add another dimension to the accessibility model by asserting that one must consider uncertain future conditions when making location decisions (Daskin & Dean, 2004). Organizational adaptability approaches incorporate tools such as scenario planning or expected value optimization models to predict future events and arrive at an optimal solution in anticipation of future conditions. The Alliance agreed that such models seemed appropriate in this clinic location-planning scenario, as local demographic or financing conditions could change even when clinic locations remained fixed. In their review of physical coverage models for primary care services, Griffin, Scherrer, and Swann (2008) suggested that demand predictors should be used in location planning. Data from the National Health and Nutrition Examination Survey conducted by the Centers for Disease Control were used to estimate the prevalence of health conditions common to the poor and uninsured by local area (CDC, 2011). The estimated demand by local area was then included in a function to minimize the total distance between areas of demand and points of service in the community.

After review of models in the literature, the Alliance group felt that existing planning models suggested proximity to client populations with demand and resources were key, but were inadequate to accommodate the community health care clinic business model, not taking into account existing capacity or consideration of public insurance programs as a vehicle for financial sustainability in the CHC organization. Thus, the group considered the results of its literature search and through a Delphi technique adopted a broader conceptual framework with the inclusion of three broad constructs – demand, capacity, and sustainability – to address stakeholder needs and help identify optimal locations for community safety net clinics. Through this discussion, the group defined its key constructs as:

Demand – factors expected to predict the use of primary care services by the poor and uninsured in the community

Capacity – viewed from a community perspective, identify where existing providers were located and minimize overlap created by newly established clinic sites

Sustainability – maximize proximity to populations that have insurance resources (inclusive of the Medicaid program for the poor).

The clinic location planning model (CLPM) therefore sought to find the optimal degree of overlap in the three constructs, as indicated by the arrow in the graphical description of the model shown in Fig. 1.

Variables included in the CLPM were selected by the Alliance, the authors, and community stakeholders using the Delphi technique. This process was not without some need for consensus building. For example, some members of the community believed that proximity to inpatient hospital services should be considered as a predictor of demand, thinking that hospital locations predicted emergency health care services. Others in the group felt that emergency hospital services were something to be avoided as an inefficient use of community resources and so felt the rate of emergency use was a better predictor of the need for preventive primary care services. After some discussion of the community resource implications of the uninsured using emergency hospital services as a substitute for preventive primary care, the group agreed to use a local rate of emergency service utilization as a predictor of the need for CHC services.

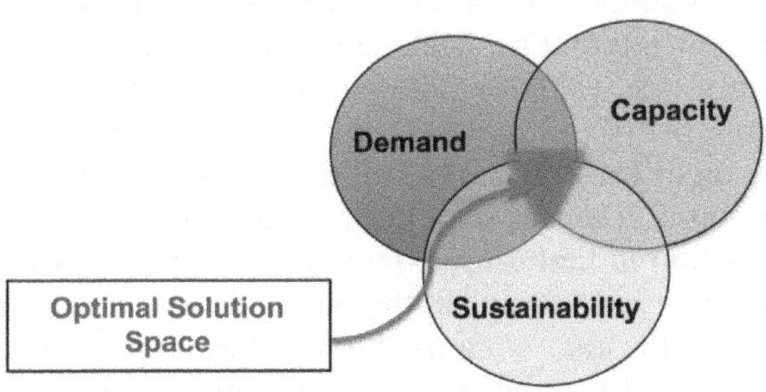

Fig. 1. Clinic Location Planning Model.

After considering input from participants, the Alliance accepted a final set of variables within each construct for the model. Participants sought variables that could be measured using publicly available, objective data that could be updated as new data are released. Consistent with previous research (Griffin et al., 2008), the unit of analysis was the United States Census Bureau (USCB) census tract. Variables in each construct were ranked based on desirability and then assigned a score. Scores for variables within each construct were then totaled and weighted into a community-specific optimal space planning equation. This analysis relied entirely on secondary data available from published sources, with no human subject involvement, and so was not subject to Institutional Review Board (IRB) review.

Demand Variables

Variables impacting demand were those expected to have an association with use of services by uninsured populations (see Table 1). Demand level factors included health care services, population and expected growth, and utilization. Increased household income is associated with higher demand for health care services (Folland, Goodman, & Stano, 2004). Data for these variables were available at the census tract level from the USCB. Emergency department utilization for primary care services was used as an indicator of the presence of uninsured populations, given the propensity of the uninsured to postpone care until an acute situation arises (Bovbjerg & Ullman, 2001; Kaiser Family Foundation, 2010). Birth rates were also used as a demand variable, since 31% of women were found to be uninsured in Texas (Kaiser Family Foundation, 2010).

Capacity Variables

Variables for the capacity construct included the presence of existing private practice physicians in the primary care specialties of family practice, general practice, or internal medicine, and the existing safety net clinic sites in Harris County (see Table 2). The physician variable in this model was based on the number of primary care physicians in an office-based practice, seeing patients on at least 50% of a full-time basis located within five miles of the center point of a census tract (a point defined by the term "centroid") per 1,000 population in that census tract. This distinction was needed based on the fact that many physicians in the public data source used were identified as part-time with other administrative duties in hospitals, health plans, or public agencies. In order to segregate physicians that represented

Table 1. Summary of Variables for Demand Construct.

Variable	Data Source	Coding
Average household expenditures for health care	2007 Federal Census Update	Published at census tract level
Population	2007 Federal Census Update	Published at census tract level
Population growth %	2000 Federal Census and 2007 Federal Census Update	Published at census tract level
Median income	2007 Federal Census Update	Published at census tract level
Median household income <200% of federal poverty level	Calculated using median household income and average household size from 2007 Federal Census Update	Published at census tract level
Medically underserved population	2009 HRSA Update	Published at census tract level
Medically underserved area	2009 HRSA Update	Published at census tract level
ER Utilization for PCP visits	2007 ER Utilization Report	Data published at zip code level. Attributes across the zip code applied to all census tracts within the zip code boundary
ER Utilization for PCP visits – Medicaid	2007 ER Utilization Report	Data published at zip code level
ER Utilization for PCP visits – SCHIP	2007 ER Utilization Report	Data published at zip code level
ER Utilization for PCP visits – Uninsured	2007 ER Utilization Report	Data published at zip code level.
# of Births	Texas Hospital Inpatient Discharge Public Use Data File (2007)	Data published at zip code level. Attributes across the zip code applied to all census tracts within the zip code boundary
% Uninsured	2007 Public Use Microdata Area (PUMA) file from Census Bureau	Data published at PUMA level, encompassing multiple census tracts, PUMA attributes applied to all encompassing tracts

existing community capacity, the stakeholder panel believed that the 50% threshold was an adequate measure of available patient care resources.

Distance served as a proxy for location within the census tract. In addition, using a distance function accounted for census tracts that did not have physicians in the census tract, but had physician offices nearby in adjacent tracts. Proximity to clinic providers is a key factor for uninsured

Table 2. Summary of Variables for Capacity Construct.

Variable	Data Source	Coding
Physicians [# of PCP in census tract/(Population/ 1,000)]	State of Texas Medical Licensing Board address of primary office location	Geocoding of all physician office addresses and calculating the distance in miles from center point of each census tract
Number of existing safety net services within 5 miles of center point of census tract	Listing of FQHC plus other safety net clinic sites	Geocoding of all clinic addresses and calculating the distance in miles from center point of each census tract

populations, given that they experience greater transportation-related challenges in access to care (Cordasco, Ponce, Gatchell, Traudt, & Escarce, 2011).

A rate per thousand was used to normalize the number of physicians in private practice to the total population in a census tract. Since data were not available to identify which physicians were seeing patients by type of insurance, it was not possible to know which physicians were serving the uninsured. As a result, an overall rate of available physician resources was used. A similar approach was used to locate existing safety net clinics within census tracts. All 96 safety net clinics in Harris County were geocoded. The distance between each clinic and each census tract in the county was calculated, resulting in 62,304 clinic/centroid pairs. Pairs totaling five miles or less were totaled for each census tract.

Sustainability Variables

Sustainability variables focused on income and insurance (see Table 3). In this construct, income was considered a predictor of eligibility for Medicaid insurance which had a multifaceted benefit to organizational sustainability. First, the prospect of expanded Medicaid eligibility under health reforms being implemented in the United States suggested that areas with low household income could transfer some uninsured persons to insured under Medicaid, thus representing a potential future financial benefit. In addition, Medicaid reimbursements to FQHC and FQHC look-alike providers are higher than for other providers for the same service, creating an incentive for these organizations to locate in areas where concentrations of poor and medically underserved patients are found (Brown & Stevens, 2006). Also, clinic locations in areas with low household income would gain favorable access to government grants to fund clinic construction. Access to such

Table 3. Summary of Variables for Sustainability Construct.

Variable	Data Source	Coding
Median income	2007 Federal Census Update	Published at census tract level
% Insured (commercial, Medicare, Medicaid, self)	2007 Public Use Microdata Area (PUMA) File from Census Bureau	Data published at PUMA level, encompassing multiple census tracts. PUMA attributes applied to all encompassed tracts

lower cost capital would ease any ongoing debt burdens of a clinic and minimize the need to divert operating surpluses to pay debt. Data for the income variable were obtained at the census tract level from 2007 USCB data. The proportion of persons with various types of insurance (Medicare, Medicaid, or commercial) was obtained from USCB annual survey data.

Weighting and Analysis

The wide dispersion of units of measure for included variables made integration of absolute values for all data points into one optimization calculation problematic. Given the diversity in units of measure, a ranking methodology was adopted. Some census tracts had very small populations (less than 100), which created unusual observations in rate-based variables, noted in 30 of 649 census tracts in Harris County. To avoid potential bias in the model from extremely high and low values, those census tracts with populations less than 100 were omitted from the model data set, leaving a final count of 619 census tracts ranked in the model.

Values for each variable were sorted low to high, with most desirable values highest. Sorted data points were then stratified into 10 groups. The top 10% of data points in each variable (those most desirable) were assigned value of 10; the next 10% of data points assigned a value of 9, and so on down to a minimum value of 1. Ranking scores for the variables in each construct were then summed to derive a score for each construct for each census tract. Each construct was assigned a relative weight to place a value for each construct in desirability for the optimized solution as described in Fig. 1 earlier, to maximize measures of demand and sustainability while minimizing competition. After discussion among the Alliance, community stakeholders, and the authors, weights used in the model described here were: 50% demand, 40% sustainability, and 10% competition, resulting in a model expressed as a mathematical function as:

$$y = 0.5(\text{Demand}) + 0.4(\text{Sustainability}) - 0.1(\text{Competition})$$

Weights for each construct were applied to the scores for that construct in each census tract. Sensitivity analysis of the model indicated little sensitivity to changes in weights. Weighted scores for each construct were then summed to arrive at a composite score, representing the solution for the relative desirability of a census tract for potential expansion of safety net capacity in Harris County.

RESULTS

Using the scoring methodology noted above, the maximum scores for each construct and the range of scores observed for 619 census tracts in Harris Country are listed in Table 4.

Composite scores for each census tract were sorted high to low and the top scoring census tracts were identified. Results for the top 10 census tracts in this example are illustrated in Table 5. Six of the 10 census tracts

Table 4. Summary of Model Scores by Construct.

Construct	Number of Variables	Maximum Score	Mean Score	High Score	Low Score
Demand	13	130	60.2	72	33
Competition	2	20	10.3	19	2
Sustainability	5	50	27.8	40	13

Table 5. Ranking of Top 10 Census Tracts Based on Composite Scores (Includes Construct Variables).

Census Tract	Composite Score	Medically Underserved Area	Household Income <200% FPL	Existing Clinic
A	51.7	Yes	Yes	No
B	50.1	Yes	Yes	No
C	49.0	Yes	Yes	No
D	48.1	Yes	Yes	No
E	48.1	Yes	Yes	No
F	47.9	No	No	No
G	47.9	No	No	No
H	47.8	No	No	No
I	47.5	Yes	Yes	No
J	47.4	No	Yes	No

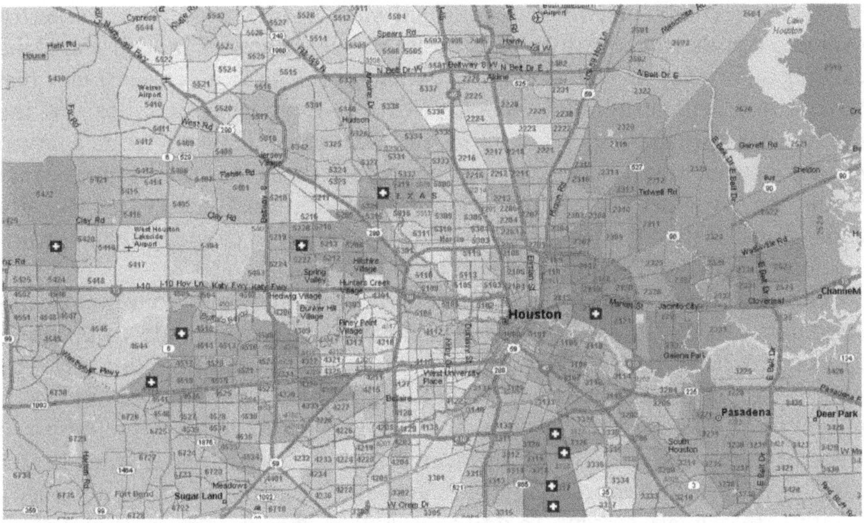

Fig. 2. Plot of CLPM Results.

with the highest composite scores were MUAs with median household incomes at or below 200% of FPL – key criterion for local areas to support an FQHC or FQHC look-alike organization. This observation seemed to demonstrate some degree of robustness in the model's ability to identify census tracts that represented potentially viable sites for establishing safety net facilities in this example.

The results of this model were plotted on a map of the Houston area and are depicted in Fig. 1. Clusters of areas with high demand, high sustainability, and low competition were readily apparent, with little overlap among them. When the location of census tracts ranked highest in the analysis was superimposed on the mapping of each construct, the logic of the solutions became apparent: the optimal locations were in areas of high demand, but proximate to areas of high sustainability with moderate impacts on existing providers. Use of a graphical presentation of model findings thus added reinforcement to the suitability of the solution (Fig. 2).

DISCUSSION

Results from the model were considered a viable first step in isolating census tracts for further evaluation as sites to expand the county's existing safety net provider network. Additional steps would need to be taken to evaluate census tracts identified as desirable based on this model. First, the existing safety net providers serving patients in or near a census tract must be assessed to determine if capacity exists in those provider sites. To the extent that a facility serves a large proportion of patients from a given nearby census tract and is operating below capacity, that census tract would be bypassed for consideration for additional safety net facility expansion. However, if that facility were operating at capacity then consideration of expanded capacity would be indicated.

This is a model that local safety net clinic planners and community stakeholders can use to analyze demographic and utilization data to optimize capacity expansion to serve uninsured and Medicaid populations. The uninsured and underserved face a challenge in access to care and limited or no ability to pay for the care received (Cunningham, 2007). Unreimbursed costs of care provided to the uninsured place a strain on existing health care providers and potentially threaten the viability of a community's health care delivery system. In addition, low Medicaid reimbursement rates and increased numbers of Medicaid enrollees will likely increase demand for CHCs. Community-based clinics for the uninsured and underserved represent a viable alternative to meeting the health care needs of this population.

The Houston setting used in this project provides an example of using consensus from community stakeholders to operationalize a rational model for identifying optimal sites for safety net clinics. With input from the local provider community, the model was able to show geographical areas that needed help, providing objective guidance for community safety net care stakeholders. In the Houston community, the model has already been put to use for a possible clinic expansion. The governing board of an existing FQHC had an interest in expanding to a nearby part of the community. The model indicated that the desired location was among the top 10 census tracts identified in Table 5 as desirable. The center administration is currently conducting a detailed assessment of potential clinic locations in the census tract identified by the model.

The approach described here using constructs identified through a collaborative process makes this model applicable in other metropolitan areas. Our model allows for easy manipulation of variables to meet different stakeholder needs in other communities. Further, the relative ranking scale used here may be too granular for some markets and may merit reconsideration based on local area conditions. However, the core idea in the model framework is adoption of a collaborative, community-based approach to define variables of concern that can then be ranked and weighted according to stakeholder needs and preferences.

CONCLUSION

This paper reviewed the development of a unique planning model to assist CHCs in making decisions about whether and where to locate additional facilities to take advantage of the new capital funding available through the ACA. The model provides a practical example of use of demographic data in a specialized strategic planning context and gives communities a collaborative framework within which to address safety net issues. In so doing, stakeholders in a local safety net delivery system can apply an evidence-based approach to their planning process. Future research will focus on generalizability to other communities, testing variables for sensitivity, and identifying other salient variables to further assist clinic planning strategies nationwide.

Over the next few years, public policy that affects CHCs will continue to evolve. CHC leadership will need tools to help guide decisions that allow their organizations to take advantage of the opportunities and meet the challenges that these policy changes will create, all within the context of their unique safety net environment. We hope that this collaborative planning model can be one such tool.

CONFLICTS OF INTEREST AND SOURCE OF FUNDING

The University of Texas School of Public Health received a grant from the Harris County Healthcare Alliance to defray the costs of developing the model described in this work. The authors have no other conflicts of interest with respect to this work.

REFERENCES

Bovbjerg, R., & Ullman, F. (2001). Health insurance and health access: Reengineering local safety nets. *Journal of Legal Medicine*, *22*, 247–262.

Brown, L., & Stevens, B. (2006). Charge of the right brigade? Communities, coverage, and care for the uninsured. *Health Affairs*, *25*(3), 150–161.

Centers for Disease Control and Prevention (CDC). (2011). *National Center for Health Statistics (NCHS). National health and nutrition examination survey data.* Hyattsville, MD: U.S. Department of Health and Human Services, Centers for Disease Control and Prevention. Retrieved from http://www.cdc.gov/nchs/nhanes/nhanes_citation.htm. Accessed on August 30, 2011.

Cordasco, K., Ponce, N., Gatchell, M., Traudt, B., & Escarce, J. (2011). English language proficiency and geographical proximity to a safety net clinic as a predictor of health care access. *Journal of Immigrant & Minority Health*, *13*(2), 260–267.

Cunningham, P. (2007). The health care safety net: What is it, what good does it do, and will it still be there when we need it? *Harvard Health Policy Review*, 8(2) 5–15.

Daskin, M. S., & Dean, L. K. (2004). Location of health care facilities. In M. Brandeay, F. Sainfort, & W. Pierskalla (Eds.), *Operations research in healthcare: A handbook of methods and applications* (pp. 43–76). Norwell, MA: Springer Science and Business Media.

Department of Health and Human Services. (2011). *Community health centers: Increasing access to affordable, cost effective, high quality care.* Retrieved from http://www.hhs.gov/news/press/2010pres/chc.html. Accessed on February 2, 2011.

Folland, S., Goodman, A., & Stano, M. (2004). *Economics of health and health care* (4th ed.). Boston, MA: Prentice Hall.

Griffin, P., Scherrer, C., & Swann, J. (2008). Optimization of community health center Locations and service offerings with statistical need estimation. *IIE transactions*, *40*, 880–892.

Harris County Healthcare Alliance. (2013). Retrieved from http://www.hchalliance.org/member-area.html. Accessed on November 25, 2013.

Health Resources and Services Administration. (2010). *Federally qualified health center look-alike guidelines and application.* Retrieved from http://bphc.hrsa.gov/policy/pin0906/pin0906.pdf. Accessed on November 15, 2010.

Hofer, A. N., Abraham, J. E., & Moscovice, I. (2011). Expansion of coverage under the patient protection and affordable care act and primary care utilization. *Milbank Quarterly*, *89*(1), 69–89.

Kaiser Family Foundation. (2010). *The uninsured: A primer.* Retrieved from http://www.kff.org/uninsured/7451.cfm. Accessed on February 14, 2010.

Kaiser Family Foundation. (March, 2012). *Medicaid and community health centers: The relationship between coverage for adults and primary care capacity in medically underserved communities.* Issue paper. Retrieved from http://kaiserfamilyfoundation.files.wordpress.com/2013/01/8293.pdf. Accessed on November 30, 1013.

Mims, S. (2006). A sustainable behavioral health program integrated with public health primary care. *Journal of Public Health Management & Practice*, *12*(5), 456–461.

National Association of Community Health Centers. (2013). *America's health centers.* Retrieved from http://www.nachc.com/client/documents/America's_CHCs_0813.pdf. Accessed on November 30, 2013.

Owen, S. H., & Daskin, M. S. (1998). Strategic facility location: A review. *European Journal of Operational Research*, *111*(3), 423–447.

Spaeder, K. E. (2010). *How to find the best location.* Retrieved from http://entrepreneur.com.startingabusiness.startupbasics/location/article73784.html. Accessed on March 29, 2010.

Toregas, C., Swain, R., ReVelle, C., & Bergman, L. (1971). The location of emergency service facilities. *Operations Research*, *19*(6), 1363–1373.

SECTION III
PHM INTEGRATING HEALTH CARE ORGANIZATIONS AND OTHER FIELDS

ANSWERING THE CALL FOR INTEGRATING POPULATION HEALTH: INSIGHTS FROM HEALTH SYSTEM EXECUTIVES

Erik L. Carlton

ABSTRACT

Purpose – *The Affordable Care Act is transforming health care practice nationwide through emphasis on population health and prevention. Health care organizations are increasingly required to address population health needs. However, they may be ill equipped to answer that call.*

Design/methodology/approach – *This study identified ways that health care organizations might better integrate public and population health efforts to better respond to this new emphasis on population health. Employing semi-structured key informant interviews, barriers to and facilitators of integration were explored and implications for health care and public health leaders were developed.*

Findings – *Participants (*n = *17) – including senior hospital executives, group practice administrators, and health department officials – identified strategies for health care and public health leaders to more*

Population Health Management in Health Care Organizations
Advances in Health Care Management, Volume 16, 115–138

ISSN: 1474-8231/doi:10.1108/S1474-823120140000016009

effectively integrate in order to achieve better performance and population health gains. These strategies and their implications are discussed.

Originality/value – *The results of this study provide important value to health care administrators leading efforts to integrate population and public health.*

Keywords: Population health; public health; health care; integration; executives

The U.S. health and health care system is highly complex. From highly advanced hospital-based medical specialties to general primary care, from state and local health departments to community-based health-oriented organizations, insurers, medical technology and pharmaceuticals companies, health profession advocacy groups and medical and health professional training programs, this broad array of actors and influencing forces has a tremendous and often incalculable effect upon efforts to improve health system performance. Often activities by these actors occur in isolation, but increasingly that isolation is breaking down. The Affordable Care Act is transforming health care practice nationwide through emphasis on population health and prevention. Health care organizations are increasingly required to address population health needs, yet they may be ill equipped to answer that call.

In the 1988 IOM report, "The Future of Public Health" (IOM, 1988), the vital importance of transdisciplinary, interorganizational partnerships in improving health systems, and population health was noted: "Organized community effort to prevent disease and promote health involves private organizations and individuals, working on their own or in partnership with the public sector" (IOM, 1988, p. 140). In 2001, an IOM report called "Crossing the Quality Chasm" clearly spelled out the shared mission of the entire health system: "All health care organizations, professional groups, and private and public purchasers should adopt as their explicit purpose to continually reduce the burden of illness, injury, and disability, and to improve the health and functioning of the people of the United States" (IOM, 2001, p. 6). The IOM's emphasis on the role of partnerships in providing, coordinating, and expanding public health services and addressing population health needs was reiterated in the 2002 IOM report "The Future of the Public's Health" (IOM, 2002), with an entire chapter of the report focused on the health care delivery system and strong recommendations for greatly increased collaboration between the public health and health care delivery systems. While the mobilization of community partnerships to identify and address community health problems is one of the 10 Essential Public Health Services (CDC, 2013), as the 2002 IOM report points out, "... the phrase ["the health care delivery system"] suggests an order, integration, and accountability that do not exist. Communication, collaboration, or systems planning among these various entities is limited and is almost incidental to their operations" (IOM, 2002, p. 213).

The American Hospital Association's (AHA) "Health for Life" initiative (American Hospital Association, 2014) was launched in 2008 in anticipation of health care reform and includes, among other things, a recognition of the need for better funding for public health, increased connectivity and sharing of population-based health information, and the importance of greater collaboration between public health and the acute care community. In April 2012, AHA's President and CEO, Richard Umbdenstock, said the following when he addressed a conference of public health systems and services researchers: "We think it's important to identify and integrate the critical interface between public health and the acute care community to build more efficient and effective systems of care" (Umbdenstock, 2012). Umbdenstock's vision for maintaining the integrity of both disciplines while finding greater opportunities for linkage and collaboration is ideal. Indeed, he calls for collaborative health research, including identifying the best collaborative models, the correct mix and timing of both patient and population health interventions, and the best array of funding – both incentives and investments – to help drive such changes.

Several studies have examined how interorganizational partnerships may influence the delivery of public health services and/or impact population health. Some have found that such partnerships can expand and improve the capacity of state and local health departments and may improve performance of state and local public health systems (Mays et al., 2004; Mays & Scutchfield, 2010; Scutchfield, Knight, Kelly, Bhandari, & Vasilescu, 2004). Others have explored the various collaborative activities undertaken by health departments and community partners (Barnes & Curtis, 2009; Barnes, Curtis, Hall-Downey, & Moonesinghe, 2012; Zahner, 2005; Zahner, Kaiser, & Kapelke-Dale, 2005). Finally, some authors have suggested the need to better measure population health outcomes (Bilheimer, 2010; Kindig, Bookse, & Remington, 2010; Parrish, 2010; Pestronk, 2010; Remington & Booske, 2011). Regardless of state or local scope, regional or national study sample, these studies consistently suggest that partnerships may indeed be an effective and powerful opportunity to enhance public health system performance and population health outcomes.

In recognition of the potential for improved population health outcomes through increased linkages between public health and primary care, the Institute of Medicine (IOM) issued a report in early 2012 entitled "Primary Care and Public Health" (IOM, 2012). Based on examples from across the country, this report outlines principles for bringing together these two distinct entities to improve performance and achieve gains in population health. These principles are: (1) having a shared goal of population health improvement, (2) engaging the community in defining and addressing population health needs, (3) leadership from across the health system that is aligned with and supports shared population health efforts, (4) ensuring sustainability, and (5) sharing, collaborative using, and analyzing data. The report advocates for greater integration between public health and primary care. Public health includes, but is not limited to governmental public health agencies, which are increasingly shifting their attention, focus, and scope to address chronic diseases as much as infectious diseases and general sanitation. Primary care was defined by the IOM for nearly two decades as, "the provision of integrated, accessible health care services by clinicians who are accountable for addressing a large majority of personal health care" (IOM, 1996, p. 1). Primary care includes mental health. The term "integration" in this context was defined as, "the linkage of programs and activities to promote overall efficiency and effectiveness and achieve gains in population health" (IOM, 2012, p. 3). The concept of linkage is perhaps the most critical notion in this model. The question arises: How do we better link public health and primary care? As a consequence of primary care practices being increasingly integrated into and defined by larger hospital-based health care systems, the salient question then becomes: How do we increase and strengthen the linkages between public health and health care? While the IOM report outlines sweeping principles and provides some illustrative examples, the report does not fully operationalize the conditions and strategies necessary to achieve a productive level of integration.

The IOM report on primary care and public health was followed just months later with a special supplemental issue of the American Journal of Public Health entirely dedicated to the proposition of integration (APHA, 2012). In this supplement, authors noted a variety of opportunities and rationale for increasingly bridging the gap between public health and health care (Grant, 2012; Koh & Tavenner, 2012; Linde-Feucht & Coulouris, 2012; Scutchfield, Michener, & Thacker, 2012). Linkages have been and can be used to promote healthy youth development (Taliaferro & Borowsky, 2012), to increase education and awareness among primary care providers about critical public health issues (Dresser et al., 2012), to enhance graduate medical education (Hemans-Henry, Greene, & Koppaka, 2012; Wells, Sarigiannis, & Boulton, 2012), and to create opportunities to link people and communities (Sweeney, Bazemore, Phillips, Etz, & Stange, 2012), among others. The challenges of creating these linkages, including the use of electronic medical records (Klompas et al., 2012) and the functions and role of Accountable Care Organizations (Gourevitch, Cannell, Boufford, & Summers, 2012), are also noted. Building on work from the past two decades, the IOM report and the supplemental issue of AJPH together make a compelling case for the potential of integrated health systems for addressing population health needs. The call for action is clear (Koo, Felix, Dankwa-Mullan, Miller, & Waalen, 2012). The strategies to do so are much more hazy.

While this call for increased integration is resounding and unequivocal, and while certain principles for facilitating integration have been set forth and examples provided, the evidence and frameworks for achieving integration are so far underdeveloped. In an effort to further research and enhance practice across the broader health system, a consortium of organizations under the leadership of the Robert Wood Johnson Foundation (RWJF) and the National Coordinating Center for Public Health Systems and Services Research (NCC PHSSR) has established a National Research Agenda for PHSSR (Consortium, 2012). One of the seminal areas of this agenda is interorganizational relationships and partnerships, including on the particularly salient question: What conditions and strategies facilitate productive interorganizational relationships and patterns of interaction among organizations that contribute to public health strategies at local, state, and national levels?

Since the role of senior leaders and decisions makers is clearly central to the framework set forth in the 2012 IOM report, the purpose of this study was to identify, through the perspectives of these senior leaders, ways that health care organizations might better integrate with public and population health experts to better respond to this new emphasis on population health. Specifically, this study sought to understand the barriers to and facilitators of greater integration or linkage between public health and health care, with the goal of moving toward clear and actionable implications for public health and health care leaders that move beyond key measures and into key processes and practices that may assure greater linkage.

METHOD

Research Design & Methodology

Regardless of position or background, the perspectives, experiences, and insights of any individuals, let alone senior public health and health care leaders, and especially related to population health and interorganizational linkages, can be difficult to fully quantify using survey or other quantitative methods. In order to capture the richness and depth of these perspectives and insights, a qualitative study methodology was developed.

Qualitative research is characterized by its occurrence in a natural (or relatively natural) setting, use of interactive and humanistic methods, its emergent and interpretive natures, a holistic view of social phenomena, and the systematic recognition and overt inclusion of researcher reflections and perspectives (Creswell, 2003). As Krefting (1991) points out, qualitative research seeks to expand upon that which is observed by explicitly including the "subjective meanings and perceptions of the subject." The aim of qualitative research is "understanding experience as nearly as possible as its participants feel it or live it" (Sherman & Webb, 1988). Use of qualitative methods may not only be very informative, but also very powerful in describing processes and lived experiences, especially those processes and experiences which ultimately inform decisions. For this reason, authors have long advocated for greater use of qualitative methods for health services research (Mays & Pope, 1995; Pope & Mays, 1995; Popay, Rogers, & Williams, 1998).

This study employed a rigorous qualitative study design that leveraged semi-structured key informant interviews with a modified snowball sampling procedure (described below). Semi-structured key informant interviews were selected to provide a focus to interviews with participants while allowing additional insights to emerge organically from the interview process, thus harvesting the richness at the heart of qualitative research.

Qualitative Rigor

Guba (1981) and Krefting (1991) advocate a four-domain model for assessing and assuring rigor in qualitative studies without compromising the richness of the naturalistic context inherent to qualitative work. This model, with more conventional quantitative rigor correlates in parentheses, includes: truth value (credibility), applicability (transferability), consistency (reliability), and neutrality (confirmability). Member-checking and reflexive field journals were used to assure truth value (credibility). These same methods were also used to acknowledge and accept the potential for researcher bias and influence on the study process, thus helping assure neutrality (confirmability) (i.e., other researchers using these same methods, questions, and participations might arrive at similar findings). Applicability (transferability) requires a depth to the data that was achieved through depth interviewing, as described above. One of the primary methods for assuring consistency (reliability) is the code-recode procedure used in this study. Finally, while biases and influence cannot be entirely eliminated from qualitative work, they can be accounted for. It is that accounting, through structuring and application of qualitative methods, along with triangulation of findings through multiple approaches, that assures both the richness and rigor of qualitative study.

Participants

Participants ($n=17$) included senior hospital executives, group practice administrators, health department officials, and leaders of various health-oriented non-profit community groups. There was a balance of male ($n=9$) and female ($n=8$) participants. The majority of participants in the study were white/Caucasian ($n=13$) with the rest black/African-American ($n=4$). Participants were from three different countries, though all currently reside and work in the United States. Broken down by job title, participants included: hospital/health center CEO ($n=4$ active, $n=1$ former/retired), hospital/health center president or other C-suite executive ($n=6$), health department director ($n=1$), other executives of health-related organizations ($n=4$), senior policy advisor to local government ($n=1$). Participants represented a total of 11 different organizations in one urban county. Among the participants were the former board chair of an internationally renowned health care improvement institution and two former state health commissioners.

Procedure

Since no previous surveys or qualitative interview guides existed or could be found at the time the study begun, it was necessary to develop a semi-structured interview guide to serve as the backbone of and assure consistency across all of the interviews conducted. Development of the interview guide was accomplished by reviewing the extant literature on integrating public health and primary care, especially the 2012 IOM report (IOM, 2012). As indicated above, the IOM report identifies five central principles for integrating public health and primary care. These themes were built into questions included in the interview guide, along with additional questions about the main barriers to and how to facilitate greater integration across the broader health system in the county and how to leverage existing system strengths and current and/or past successes in collaboration and integration. Also included was a sweeping visioning question that allowed participants to imagine changes they would make, if so empowered, to ensure a greater level of integration among public health and health care organizations. Ultimately a list of 17 questions was created. This list was subsequently distilled down to a group of five core questions asked of all participants with the other questions available to the researcher to explore other concepts in greater depth. Example questions from the interview guide are included in the appendix. True to the nature and process of semi-structured interviews, the researcher was free to and often did ask more detailed questions to clarify and deepen participants' responses. Some have called this "active interviewing" (Holstein & Gubrium, 1993) or "depth interviewing" (Patton, 1987). Interviews varied in length from just under half an hour (26 minutes) to just over one hour (1 hour and 13 minutes).

This study used a modified snowball sampling procedure, with purposeful pre-selection of certain critical potential participants and identification of additional potential participants through the recommendation of those who participated in earlier interviews. The rationale for this modified sampling procedure was that with a focused study topic in a targeted metropolitan area, it was well known who certain key participants were and contextually assumed that their perspective was vital to understanding the questions at the heart of the study within the context of the local health system. This method proved effective and beneficial for facilitating the research process. In one case, one participant made critical connections between the researcher and additional participants by leveraging his personal connection with three senior hospital executives to invite and encourage them to participate.

For a variety of reasons, some potential participants ($n = 9$) who were identified by those who completed interviews were not interviewed for this study. Reasons included no response to email and phone invitations to participate in the study or lack of accurate contact information provided by previous participants. However, the main reason these participants were not included or pursued further was that saturation – a key element of qualitative research that is discussed below – was perceived by the researcher to have been achieved.

The study was conducted with the approval of The University of Memphis Institutional Review Board and all participants were consented prior to interviews beginning. All interviews were recorded, with the permission of study participants provided under the signed consent, for transcription and analysis.

Analysis

Transcription of the recorded interviews were completed and checked for accuracy. Given the emergent, organic nature of qualitative research, data analysis is a highly reflective process for the researcher (Creswell, 2003). A reflexive field journal (Krefting, 1991) was used to record the researcher's reactions to each interview, the themes which seemed to be developing across multiple participants, and the researcher's own personal thoughts and reflections. These processes allowed the researcher to recall aspects of each interview, and identify potential biases that could have colored the research. These notes also served as the initial coding structure for qualitative analysis. Transcripts were then reviewed and further codes were developed and tested through a code-recode procedure. This procedure, which helps ensure data reliability, involved initially coding a portion of the interview data then returning to the data at a later date and recoding it. The results of these codings were compared to be sure coding was performed consistently. Once a coding structure was formalized, all transcripts were analyzed and coded.

As initial themes and concepts emerged from the data analysis, a member-checking procedure (Ellis & Bochner, 2000; Krefting, 1991) was also used. This procedure involved providing data to research participants for comments and further response, as well as asking later participants about themes suggested by earlier participants in the study. Essentially, the study participants were the ones who validated the study findings.

All quotations shared herein are direct quotations from participants. Only minor grammatical revisions have been made. Names (and positions where necessary) are removed to ensure confidentiality.

RESULTS

Participants provided a rich variety of perspectives about the barriers to and facilitators of greater linkage between public health and health care. Analysis of the interview transcripts combined with research notes revealed that all participants ($n = 17$) identified a common set of barriers and facilitative strategies for health care and public health leaders to more effectively link their organizational activities in order to achieve better performance and population health gains. This set of barriers and strategies includes (1) focusing on targeted issues with shared interest among all parties, (2) building on current and past success in collaborating, (3) leveraging payers and business partners to expand support for integrated models, (4) training and retraining the public health and health care workforce (including both administrative and technical/clinical staff) with the knowledge and skills necessary for interdisciplinary work, (5) harnessing market forces and health care reform as key drivers, and (6) developing and supporting a strong convening agency (Fig. 1).

Focus on Targeted Issues with Shared Interest

Participants were quick to point out that the concept of integrating public health and health care is much too broad to be tackled generally. Confusion, competition, diffusion of responsibilities, and lack of resources or energy or will, can all quickly derail efforts to bring together the many players in a given community's broader health system. However, breaking integration down into smaller steps and focusing specific issues can provide a necessary focus to bring stakeholders together. One executive of a community-based non-profit that brings together a number of different

1. Focus on targeted issues with shared interest
2. Build on current and past success collaborating
3. Leverage payers and business partners to expand support for integrated models
4. Train/retraining the healthcare workforce
5. Harness market forces and healthcare reform as key drivers
6. Develop and support a strong convening agency.

Fig. 1. Key Themes.

agencies said, "Special project work on specific issues can be key. Some funders even mandate collaboration." Another participant, working for a different community-based group, added that finding areas where most, if not all, parties are struggling could be excellent motivation for participation. In relation to development of efforts around a specific health issue, in this case hypertension, this participant suggested the overall tone among partners was, "Why are we competing on this? No one is doing a particularly stellar job."

One participant, a former hospital CEO, was quite clear as to how the competitive divide can be bridged in the interest of issues that affect all stakeholders: "A marriage between clinical medicine and public health is needed. We need to get beyond who has the better billboard. We can compete on the clinical determinants of health and collaborate on the non-clinical determinants, pooling resources and investments." Given this, it is important for health care and public health leaders to identify where competition exists and where they do not so as to guide broader community-based efforts.

Build on Success

In addition to finding areas of common interest, participants suggested that momentum could be gained by building on current and past successes. One said, "We need to work on the achievables, get small wins." Another provided greater detail to this same notion: "We have a history of this – community-based clinics, early success and breastfeeding coalitions, infant mortality, end of life care, hypertension collaborative, even domestic violence in the past. We've done this. We are doing this. People are at the table. We can build on this and do more." Recognizing strengths in the systems and building on them to achieve more can reduce the need to reinvent the collaborative wheel. Many communities, like the one studied, likely have a history of organizations coming together and accomplishing things, perhaps even in the health and health care sector. Current and recent efforts can be supported, reinforced, and re-energized to serve as the engine and framework for on-going and expanded collaborative efforts.

Leverage Payers and Business Partners to Expand Support

"We need greater investment. We're still dependent on the goodwill of a lot of people, and I don't know how long we can maintain that," lamented a director of a non-profit community-based group working on health issues, "We're convening healthcare giants with miniscule resources." Even well-targeted, meaningful initiatives that build on past successes can sputter and fail under the weight of managing multiple agencies and their participating representatives. Additionally, a conception of health in a community that is limited to only health care and public health is not only short-sighted, it is also fundamentally incorrect. One participant, who leads a non-profit group of organizations interested in health issues, offered the following thought: "We need a broader definition of who's involved in changing health. Health care is the smallest percentage of those with influence. What about education? What about business and economic development? We need to get out of silos and have a whole cadre of people who care."

Still, some organizations and participants feel there is almost a moral-driven value set that suggests they should be compelled to work together, to do more. This idea can run quite contrary to the fiscal and operational realities organizations face. "There are lots of 'oughts' in the system, but there is a difference between what we ought to do and what we can do. Money is the key. Economic incentives and disincentives are not in place to drive population health effort," offered one community health center executive. Without the right incentives and disincentives, the justification to collaborate and integrate interorganizationally can be limited. The role of businesses, insurance companies, and other "third party players and payers" can be significant in overcoming the competitive and collaborative inertia that can exist within efforts to better integrate public health and health care. As one health care executive noted, "Competition can be lessened when the third party payers come to the table."

Train and Retrain the Workforce

Perhaps the most challenging aspect of integration pointed out by participants was that we simply do not have a workforce in health care or public health that is trained to work and speak and collaborate across disciplinary boundaries. Health care executives know all too well the difficulties of engaging administrative and clinical staff in a cogent and productive conversation. Adding in other disciplines and entire agencies with people who are trained to act and think differently adds a level of challenge that may not be readily accomplished by forcing people around the table together. One participant said, "Public health has never been the role of the hospitals. In medicine, you're not trained to think that way and, certainly, it's just not how the system is structured. So it takes some really forward thinking people to do that." Or, as another suggested, "We're simply not trained to work across the divide."

Consequently, and as suggested by participants, it may well be time to fundamentally redesign how we train and retrain the health care and public health workforces. One participant was quiet clear, "Public health and healthcare do not have the same language and they do not get the same training. Do we re-think education so we can create more bridges? What do we really want and need our people to know?" We can enhance public health and medical training with the shared language of population health, as well as a better understanding of how each side's individual actions can contribute to each other and to improve overall population health.

This may start on the public health side of things. Public health is a largely nebulous concept that can be conceptualized at once as a specific governmental agency or set of agencies with specific mandates and statutory responsibilities and also a general theoretical approach that involves a broad set of disciplines. Perhaps public health has failed to clearly define itself as a profession. "The average person, the average provider, they just don't understand public health – what it does, the value of its services. Public health is often just seen as stop gap services. It's hard to value something so ambiguous." Further, while efforts by students to slap stickers on everything remotely related to public health can serve as an import public awareness campaign, never mind the question of cleanup, it may well only provide a greater level of confusion. Just as public health professionals and executives can do a better job of clarifying who and what they are, so too can health care executives by reaching out proactively across the divide to better understand what public health is and what it might offer to their organization's efforts to improve the health of both individuals and populations. Notably, a hospital executive and former state health commissioner said the following, "Public health needs to quit talking to itself. Health care needs to quit talking to itself. Our successes are when we start talking to others. We need to speak in a language the other understands."

Perhaps it is time for a vision of a highly trained workforce with the skills, abilities, and desire to think, and work innovatively. "Better patient outcomes, better system performance and better professional development are all inextricably linked," replied one former hospital CEO and former board chair of a renowned international health care improvement agency, "We need more who understand, who really get population health and we need more leadership in the new order. We're spending so much money in the wrong way. We need young, civic – not corporate – leaders. We need an insurgency. We need people trained in population health and metrics."

Harness Market Forces and Health Care Reform

The call for integrating public health and health care is occurring at a time when health care reform is transforming the very fabric of both medicine and public health. The changes in the market economy around health and health care, along with shifts in funding for public health, and new mandates for health care and provisions for public health under the Affordable Care Act can be harnessed to transform how health care and public health agencies conduct business, including the justification for greater integration.

Finances are clearly one of the biggest obstacles to collaboration. One participant stated that, "Unless payment reform really does happen, I don't see hospitals working that hard to keep people out of the hospital." Another offered this: "Finances create artificial barriers. One of the great challenges we have is mal-aligned incentives for doing the right thing." So there must be a clear and compelling financial rationale for organizations to work together. One participant, a former state health commissioner, said, "The Triple Aim, CMS, and the ACA all provide incentives and opportunities, carrots and sticks, to improve population health. It's not just about being good corporate citizens. Now there is a business case for hospitals to do more. Value-based reimbursement – the carrot – and readmission penalties – the stick – encourage better integration. This policy shift institutionalizes the business case. ACA is the framework and infrastructure, a catalyst, to accelerate intentionality."

Develop and Support a Strong Convening Agency

Perhaps no concept is more central to any collaborative effort, more ubiquitous in literature across the collaborative sciences, than an utter necessity of having a strong and enduring convener to bring together the variety of agencies and actors the compromise the breadth of influential activity in a given sphere. "There has to be some sort of formal or informal structure, a convener or connector, to bring people together to talk, to create a shared goal and aims." For health and health care, this breadth can be quite immense and powerful. From hospital-based health care systems to local governmental public health agencies, insurers, businesses and other payers, any number of small or large community groups focused on health issues, the sheer volume of activity in any given community related to health can be overwhelming. A convener is critical. "There needs to be a shared space to create shared goals, a neutral forum for being open and honest, a place with some sort of centralizing function, some sort of collaborative gravity, where collaboration can become more organized, more emergent, a place that is not anyone's entity, but one created by the people at the table, who created the conversation." Without a strong, neutral body at the hub of this activity, systemic entropy is a nearly assured phenomenon.

DISCUSSION

Several simple suggestions for enhanced integration emerged from this study. From leveraging the role of businesses, insurers, and other payers, to training the public health and health care workforces to work the interdisciplinary divide, there are several relevant takeaways from this study.

Perhaps the most salient and germane is to step away from thinking about wholesale system-wide collaboration of all players on all issues and move toward more targeted, issue-specific efforts that leverage key players and organizations to address problems encountered by all or most. Many localities have previously come together to address a variety of issues. Building on existing and past successes can be a powerful jumpstart to future shared work. A shared goal of population health starts with a shared goal for one health outcome. A strong convening agency, well positioned and well resourced at the hub of health care and public health activities, can bring together and facilitate the interactions and efforts of health care, public health, businesses, insurers, and other stakeholders with a neutrality that can temper competition and a focus that can breed engagement, investment, innovation, and action.

Recently, the de Beaumont Foundation partnered with the Centers for Disease Control and Prevention and the Department of Community and Family Medicine at Duke University to develop an interactive, web-enabled tool to assist in efforts to integrate health care and public health in communities (de Beaumont Foundation, 2014). This tool, which is called *Public Health and Primary Care Together: A Practical Playbook*, aims to provide a comprehensive approach, complete with practical tools for integration, with the hope of transforming the relationship between the public health and primary care sectors. While an evaluation of its effectiveness has yet to be conducted, tools such as this, guided by the fundamental principles outlined in the 2012 IOM report and informed by concepts like those identified in this study, may have a powerful effect on the efficacy of integration efforts.

Even with practical tools in place, the results of this study suggest that integrating public health with health care will ultimately require the will and motivation of individuals and leaders of organizations in individual communities to change the landscape of population health and ensure a more functional, effective health system.

The several themes identified above lead to a number of important implications for health care executives. One of the most challenging implications of this research and the general area of practice and inquiry it informs is that of balancing organizational operational missions and resources with new population health requirements. Health care executives are ultimately responsible for the management and performance of their respective organizations. Stepping outside of normal operational procedures and long-established strategic requirements can be discomforting at best and seemingly unreasonable, irresponsible, or near impossible at worst. Leaders deeply understand that overcoming the inertia of myopic organizational thinking can require significant effort. It can be all too facile for health care executives and other organizational decision makers to perceive and dismiss population and public health interventions as unnecessary or ultimately superfluous activities that distract from the operational imperatives of the health care organization. Efforts in the integration sphere require a dual comfort with less measurable deliverables and uncustomary terminology and approaches. Engagement with public health to provide a more integrated population health approach thus requires both a clear and compelling business rationale and a willingness to work through the discomforts of new conceptual tools and processes implicit to this shared interdisciplinary space.

Health care reform, including shifts to value-based reimbursement and community benefit (where applicable), has provided the fertile ground in which to sow new integrated approaches. Since both incorporation status (for many) and income streams (for all) now rely on this newer population-based approach, leaders must account for these forces and consider methods for enhancing how their organization(s) approach these requirements. Leaders of health systems and health care organizations could explore opportunities to overlap competitive strategy with this community benefit so that both agency and community needs are addressed.

Community benefit requirements can be seen merely as a box to check – "We have done our community needs assessment this year, so we're free and clear for another two." – rather than an opportunity to expand the organization's presence in the community and leverage findings to enhance market share and competition advantages.

Also, some health care organizations may be tempted to try and develop a new set of competencies internally. While this may be effective to a limited extent in adjusting the extant direct service delivery medical model that has been central to health care in the United States for well over a century, it may also be mistaken to try and in-house all competencies. Such an attempt could lead to overinvestment of organizational resources when investment of human, financial, and physical resources on a smaller, but more targeted and collaborative scale – such as efforts that deliberatively and intentionally engage individuals and organizations with population health skill sets – may well be much more fruitful. Investments like these require individual leaders and their organizations to let go of complete control for certain outcomes, which in turn requires trust in others along with a dedication to seeing the collaboration through its inevitable ups and downs.

There is certainly more rationale for answering the call for integration than direct financial justifications. Shared activities that can be leveraged to enhance strategic initiatives and competitive advantages can provide enough rationale for leaders to involve their organization in broader public and population health activities. Participation in the public sphere may provide direct financial and procedural benefits, and establish a health care organization's role and strategic position within the community. Health care organizations which have been previously ridiculed for their focus on profits over people and community, or haunted by previous decisions to move facilities or jobs into other areas of certain communities, can find local opinions of their organizations softened and ameliorated by their engagement with the broader community. Hospitals and health care organizations may grow as a result of their involvement with public health in efforts that benefit the community at large.

Further, health care executives can also identify areas in which collaboration is more favorable than competition, perhaps where no strong competitive advantage exists for any individual organization and where all would be benefitted by joint participation to address shared issues. As suggested by one of the participants in this study (quoted above): compete on the clinicals, collaborate on the non-clinicals. In these circumstances, health care leaders should not be shy about engaging with public health, and other health care executives and organizations. Participating on health councils comprised of cross-sectional representatives and led by a more neutral agency, such as a health department or academic institution, is one approach that can be effectively employed. Health care executives might also proactively engage other health care, public health, and community-based organizational leaders in conversations to establish a shared common ground for greater collaboration and integration. Conducting shared community needs assessments and developing shared intervention plans can greatly reduce duplication of efforts, inefficiencies, and confusion where multiple health care organizations operate. For example, in a city where multiple hospitals aligned with three major health care systems, multiple community health centers, a federally qualified health center or multiple such centers, the local health department, and local health-oriented community groups all conduct their own community needs assessment, wasted effort, and a significant amount of overlap is likely. Developing and/or engaging a strong convening agency, as noted above, such as a graduate school of public health or a population health institute, can serve all partners more effectively than each of these agencies attempting their own efforts. This may also have the additional benefit of greater community participation, as community leaders from other sectors, as well as residents, have a clearer picture of what is being done across the community.

Limitations

While the sample size ($n = 17$) may seem small by quantitative standards, the robustness and power of the findings can be found in the consistency and resonance of the themes identified by all participants and the triangulation accomplished by use of multiple analytical methods to ensure rigor. Still, limitations to the methodology exist. Multi-rater coding is an analytical method where multiple researchers analyze the transcripts of interviews to develop and deploy a shared coding scheme. Since a single researcher conducted this study, this method was not available. However, other methods used (as described earlier) help to triangulate findings and account for the presence of research bias. Additionally, not all leaders were originally targeted or subsequently recommended for participation in this study. Lack of complete participation by all identified potential research subjects may be seen as a limitation by some, especially given the sample size. However, one of the central components of qualitative research is saturation, that point at which the qualitative process yields no new findings.

During the course of 17 interviews, and through the ensuing analysis and member checking, it became quite evident that saturation had been reached. For this reason, interviews were discontinued. It is certainly possible that additional participants may have contributed further insight, so this remains a limitation implicit to the qualitative process. However, as stated above, use of multiple methods and the achievement of saturation should assuage some of the concern of this limitation. Finally, qualitative themes can be tested, validated and strengthened, or refuted through quantitative methods. Not having mixed-method findings is a limitation of this study. However, this does afford an opportunity for further research into this topic.

Implications for Future Research

This study offers a number of additional opportunities for future research. There is an implicit assumption in the literature and policies related to integration that better integration lowers costs and improves health outcomes. It is increasingly important to find ways to test and validate this assumption. Measures of population health and the influence thereon can be challenging. Therefore, rigorous methodological studies will be required to truly drive at the economics and financials of integration. Related to this, we need to study the return on investment (ROI) for integration efforts. How can ROI be measured for population-level health outcomes? How does that translate to the individual participating organizations that helped pull it off? How is the payoff to be known? Is there a critical level of investment relative to community size or population characteristics? All of these are critical questions related to the field of public health and health care integration.

FINAL THOUGHTS

Unlike other goods or services, health and health care inhabit a relatively unique position within the scope of individual and community needs. Perhaps more than any other sector of society health care and public health have profound, durable influences on the health and well-being of both individuals and populations. For this reason, the ethical and moral ramifications of actions undertaken by health care executives and their public health peers have far greater import and, as a consequence, merit far greater consideration, intention, and interorganizational collaboration than leading actors in other industries. Such a conception could not have been captured any more clearly or expressed any more powerfully than the simple sentiment shared by one health care executive who participated in this study:

> At some level, we have both a moral and an economic imperative to change how the system works: An *economic imperative* to save money, reduce costs and waste, and a *moral imperative* to both save lives and improve health ... Those with a *democratic imperative* for a given population must own it.

ACKNOWLEDGMENTS

The advice and mentorship of Dr. Paul Erwin at the University of Tennessee – Knoxville was central to the success of this study.

This study was made possible by funding from the Robert Wood Johnson Foundation through the National Coordinating Center for Public Health Systems and Services Research (NCC PHSSR), and through the constant encouragement and technical support provided by Dr. Doug Scutchfield, Mrs. Cynthia Lamberth, Mrs. Erin Louis, and other staff at the national coordinating center.

Above all, the contributions and insights provided by study participants cannot be underappreciated. Their candor and willingness to share their perspective is what made this study meaningful.

REFERENCES

American Hospital Association. (2014). *Health for life: Better health. better health care.* Retrieved from http://www.aha.org/advocacy-issues/healthforlife/index.shtml. Accessed on March 4, 2014.

APHA. (2012). Integrating primary care and public health. *American Journal of Public Health, 102*(Suppl. 3).

Barnes, P. A., & Curtis, A. B. (2009). A national examination of partnerships among local health departments and faith communities in the U.S. *Journal of Public Health Management and Practice, 15*(3), 253–263.

Barnes, P. A., Curtis, A. B., Hall-Downey, L., & Moonesinghe, R. (2012). A multistate examination of partnership activity among local public health systems using the National Public Health Performance Standards. *Journal of Public Health Management and Practice, 18*(5), E14–E23.

Bilheimer, L. T. (2010). Evaluating metrics to improve population health. *Preventing Chronic Disease*, *7*(4), A69.

CDC. (2013). *The public health system and the 10 essential public health services*. Retrieved from http://www.cdc.gov/nphpsp/essentialservices.html

Consortium. [A consortium from Altarum Institute, the Centers for Disease Control and Prevention, the Robert Wood Johnson Foundation, and the National Coordinating Center for Public Health Services and Systems Research]. (2012). A national research agenda for public health services and systems. *American Journal of Preventive Medicine*, *42*(5S1), S72–S78.

Creswell, J. W. (2003). *Research design: Qualitative, quantitative, and mixed methods approaches* (2nd ed.). Thousand Oaks, CA: Sage.

de Beaumont Foundation. (2014). *Public health and primary care together: A practical playbook*. Retrieved from http://www.practicalplaybook.org/. Accessed on March 3, 2014.

Dresser, M. G., Short, L., Wedemeyer, L., Bredow, V. L., Sacks, R., Larson, K., … Silver, L. D. (2012). Public health detailing of primary care providers: New York city's experience, 2003–2010. *American Journal of Public Health*, *102*(S3), S342–S352. doi:10.2105/AJPH.2011.300622

Ellis, C., & Bochner, A. P. (2000). Autoethnography, personal narrative, reflexivity: Researcher as subject. In N. K. Denzin & Y. S. Lincoln (Eds.), *Handbook of qualitative research* (2nd ed., pp. 733–768). Thousand Oaks, CA: Sage.

Gourevitch, M. N., Cannell, T., Boufford, J. I., & Summers, C. (2012). The challenge of attribution: Responsibility for population health in the context of accountable care. *American Journal of Public Health*, *102*(S3), S322–S324. doi:10.2105/AJPH.2011.300642

Grant, R. (2012). A bridge between public health and primary care. *American Journal of Public Health*, *102*(S3), S304–S304. doi:10.2105/AJPH.2012.300825

Guba, E. G. (1981). Criteria for assessing the trustworthiness of naturalistic inquiries. *Educational Resources Information Center Annual Review*, *29*, 75–91.

Hemans-Henry, C., Greene, C. M., & Koppaka, R. (2012). Integrating public health-oriented e-learning into graduate medical education. *American Journal of Public Health*, *102*(S3), S353–S356. doi:10.2105/AJPH.2012.300669

Holstein, J. A., & Gubrium, J. F. (1993). Active interviewing. In D. Silverman (Ed.), *Interpreting qualitative data: Methods for analyzing talk, text, and interaction*. London: Sage.

IOM. (1988). *The future of public health*. Washington, DC: National Academy Press.

IOM. (1996). *Primary care: America's health in a new era*. Washington, DC: National Academy Press.

IOM. (2001). *Crossing the quality chasm: A new health system for the 21st century*. Washington, DC: National Academies Press.

IOM. (2002). *The future of the public's health in the 21st century*. Retrieved from: http://www.iom.edu/Object.File/Master/4/165/AssuringFINAL.pdf. Accessed on February 13, 2010.

IOM. (2012). *Primary care and public health: Exploring integration to improve population health*. Washington, DC: The National Academies Press.

Kindig, D. A., Bookse, B. C., & Remington, P. L. (2010). Mobilizing action towards community health (MATCH): Metrics, incentives, and partnerships for population health. *Preventing Chronic Disease*, *7*(4), A68.

Klompas, M., McVetta, J., Lazarus, R., Eggleston, E., Haney, G., Kruskal, B. A., ... Platt, R. (2012). Integrating clinical practice and public health surveillance using electronic medical record systems. *American Journal of Public Health, 102*(S3), S325–S332. doi:10.2105/AJPH.2012.300811

Koh, H. K., & Tavenner, M. (2012). Connecting care through the clinic and community for a healthier America. *American Journal of Public Health, 102*(S3), S305–S307. doi:10.2105/AJPH.2012.300760

Koo, D., Felix, K., Dankwa-Mullan, I., Miller, T., & Waalen, J. (2012). A call for action on primary care and public health integration. *American Journal of Public Health, 102*(S3), S307–S309. doi:10.2105/AJPH.2012.300824

Krefting, L. (1991). Rigor in qualitative research: The assessment of trustworthiness. *American Journal of Occupational Therapy, 45*(3), 214–222.

Linde-Feucht, S., & Coulouris, N. (2012). Integrating primary care and public health: A strategic priority. *American Journal of Public Health, 102*(S3), S310–S311. doi:10.2105/AJPH.2012.300849

Mays, G. P., McHugh, M. C., Shim, K., Perry, N., Halverson, P. K., Lenaway, D., & Moonesinge, R. (2004). Identifying dimensions of performance in local public health systems: Results from the national public health performance standards program. *Journal of Public Health Management and Practice, 10*(3), 193–203.

Mays, G. P., & Scutchfield, F. D. (2010). Improving public health system performance through multi-organizational partnerships. *Preventing Chronic Disease, 10*(6).

Mays, N., & Pope, C. (1995). Rigour and qualitative research. *British Medical Journal, 311*, 109–112.

Parrish, R. G. (2010). Measuring population health outcomes. *Preventing Chronic Disease, 7*(4), A70.

Patton, M. Q. (1987). *How to use qualitative methods in evaluation*. London: Sage.

Pestronk, R. M. (2010). Using metrics to improve population health. *Preventing Chronic Disease, 7*(4), A70.

Popay, J., Rogers, A., & Williams, G. (1998). Rational and standards for the systematic review of qualitative literature in health services research. *Qualitative Health Research, 8*(3), 341–351.

Pope, C., & Mays, N. (1995). Reaching the parts other methods cannot reach: An introduction to qualitative methods in health and health services research. *British Medical Journal, 311*, 42–45.

Remington, P. L., & Booske, B. C. (2011). Measuring the health of communities: How and why? *Journal of Public Health Policy and Practice, 17*(5), 397–400.

Scutchfield, F. D., Michener, J. L., & Thacker, S. B. (2012). Are we there yet? Seizing the moment to integrate medicine and public health. *American Journal of Public Health, 102*(S3), S312–S316. doi:10.2105/AJPH.2012.300724

Scutchfield, F. D., Knight, E. A., Kelly, A. V., Bhandari, M. W., & Vasilescu, I. P. (2004). Local public health agency capacity and its relationship to public health systems performance. *Journal of Public Health Management and Practice, 10*(3), 204–215.

Sherman, R., & Webb, R. (1988). *Qualitative research in education: Focus and methods*. London: Falmer Press.

Sweeney, S. A., Bazemore, A., Phillips, R. L., Etz, R. S., & Stange, K. C. (2012). A reemerging political space for linking person and community through primary health care. *American Journal of Public Health, 102*(S3), S336–S341. doi:10.2105/AJPH.2011.300553

Taliaferro, L. A., & Borowsky, I. W. (2012). Beyond prevention: Promoting healthy youth development in primary care. *American Journal of Public Health, 102*(S3), S317–S321. doi:10.2105/AJPH.2011.300559

Umbdenstock, R. (2012). Keynote address. *Paper presented at the Public Health Systems & Services Research Keeneland Conference*, Lexington, KY.

Wells, E. V., Sarigiannis, A. N., & Boulton, M. L. (2012). Assessing integration of clinical and public health skills in preventive medicine residencies: Using competency mapping. *American Journal of Public Health, 102*(S3), S357–S367. doi:10.2105/AJPH.2012.300753

Zahner, S. J. (2005). Local public health system partnerships. *Public Health Reports, 120*(1), 76–83.

Zahner, S. J., Kaiser, B., & Kapelke-Dale, J. (2005). Local partnerships for community assessment and planning. *Journal of Public Health Management & Practice, 11*(5), 460–464.

APPENDIX: SAMPLE SEMI-STRUCTURED INTERVIEW GUIDE QUESTIONS

- What are the main barriers you see to greater integration between public health and primary care?
- In your mind, what factors would facilitate greater integration between public health and primary care?
- Do you believe that population health is a shared goal of public health, primary care, and health system organizations in Shelby County? Why or why not? How can it become more of a focus and shared goal? What impact might that have on integration?
- In what ways are we or can we better engage members of the community, as well as leaders within the health system, to identify and address population health needs?
- How are we or how can we better align leaders from across the broader health system to invest more fully in integrating health systems and services?
- If you were fully empowered to do anything you needed to assure better integration between public health and primary care, as well as across the broader health system (health care systems, public health, Healthy Shelby, etc.), what would you do?

POPULATION HEALTH MANAGEMENT IN INTEGRATED PHYSICAL AND MENTAL HEALTH CARE

Cynthia J. Sieck, Thomas Wickizer and Laurel Geist

ABSTRACT

Purpose – *Individuals suffering from serious mental illness (SMI) face many challenges of navigating a complex and often fragmented health care system and may die significantly earlier from co-morbid physical health conditions. Integrating mental and physical health care for individuals with SMI is an emerging trend addressing the often-neglected physical health care needs of this population to better coordinate care and improve health outcomes.*

Design/methodology/approach – *Population Health Management (PHM) provides a useful framework for designing integrated care programs for individuals with SMI.*

Findings – *This paper examines the structure and evolution of the integrated care program in Missouri in the context of PHM, highlighting*

Population Health Management in Health Care Organizations
Advances in Health Care Management, Volume 16, 139–150

ISSN: 1474-8231/doi:10.1108/S1474-823120140000016006

particular elements of PHM that facilitate and support development of an integrated mental and physical health care program.

Originality/value – *As health care reform provides external motivation to provide integrated care, this study can be useful as other states attempt to address this important issue.*

Keywords: Mental health services; health care services; care integration

INTRODUCTION

Individuals suffering from serious mental illness (SMI) face many challenges of navigating a complex and often fragmented health care system. While they may receive treatment for their mental health issues, their physical health problems and chronic illness may go untreated (Colton & Manderscheid, 2006; Druss, Zhao, Von Esenwein, Morrato, & Marcus, 2011; Kilbourne et al., 2009; Parks, Svendsen, Singer, Foti, & Mauer, 2006; Roshanaei-Moghaddam & Katon, 2009). National studies document a high prevalence of chronic illness and increased risk of premature mortality among individuals with SMI (Collins, Tranter, & Irvine, 2012; Colton & Manderscheid, 2006; Farnam, Zipple, Tyrrell, & Chittinanda, 1999; Kilbourne et al., 2009; Roshanaei-Moghaddam & Katon, 2009). The structure of the mental health care system varies by state and often by county within the state. Care is often provided through community mental health centers (CMHCs) with responsibility to provide care for all individuals with very limited resources (Wickizer et al., 2011).

In recent years, a trend toward providing care that integrates mental and physical health care needs has been gaining momentum at every level of the system. In some states, this trend reflects a response to components of the Patient Protection and Affordable Care Act (PP-ACA) and its push toward creating patient-centered medical homes (Croft & Parish, 2013; Garfield, Zuvekas, Lave, & Donohue, 2011; Mechanic, 2012). Under the PP-ACA, states submit a state plan amendment to the Centers for Medicare and Medicaid (CMS) for their Medicaid program to establish health homes. This would serve to "integrate and coordinate all primary, acute, behavioral health, and long-term services and supports to treat the whole person" (Medicaid.gov, 2014). To accomplish this goal, health homes provide a defined set of services including comprehensive care management, care coordination, health promotion, transitional care, patient and family support, and referrals for social support services. For the first 2 years of operation, designated health homes receive an enhanced Federal Medical Assistant Percentage which is set at 90% of the cost of these services, compared to 65% for non-health homes (Medicaid.gov, 2014). Thus, states have a strong motivation to develop health homes for their Medicaid population.

Integrated care, provided within and outside of health homes, can take a variety of forms ranging from colocation of mental and physical health care providers to collaborative efforts between both types of providers, generally coordinated by mental health providers for individuals with SMI (Druss et al., 2011; Horvitz-Lennon, Kilbourne, & Pincus, 2006; Kilbourne et al., 2009; Wickizer et al., 2011). This structure holds promise for addressing all the health care needs of individuals with SMI in an environment where they are comfortable. Mental health professionals possess a level of experience and comfort with the needs of this population that may not be present in primary care provider offices (Wickizer et al., 2011). However, addressing the physical health care needs in a mental health agency frequently represents an additional and often entirely new area of focus for MH providers. Integrated mental and physical health care requires providers to look at care in new and different ways, including the use of different metrics of care. Population health management can be a useful tool for organizations implementing an integrated care program.

What is Population Health Management?

Population Health Management (PHM) is a systematic means of addressing the health of a population, often relying on data that is collected and reported electronically and the implementation of health improvement strategies for individuals. Key to PHM is a focus on the health of a defined target population, assessed and monitored regularly through established metrics. PHM approaches the individual in a holistic manner, implementing specific strategies aimed to improve overall health (Institute for Health Technology Transformation, 2012; McAlearney, 2002).

In the integrated care arena, PHM is a useful approach for implementing an IC program. Because of the mental and physical health care needs of individuals with SMI, they are a high-risk and often high-cost population, thus presenting a good fit for PHM programs. PHM provides a structure for organizations to utilize as they design their program and often redesign job tasks. It also helps to addresses fragmentation in the system by defining the whole health of the population as everyone's job. Particularly for individuals with SMI, a PHM approach identifies strategies for addressing chronic disease management for a population in which this has been neglected (Druss et al., 2011; Kilbourne et al., 2009).

This paper examines the case of integrated care provision in the Missouri Health Home model in the context of PHM. Through a qualitative analysis of the history and evolution of integrated care in Missouri, we describe the significance of particular elements of PHM and how they facilitate and support development of an integrated mental and physical health care program.

METHODS

We conducted a detailed case study of the integrated care efforts underway in Missouri utilizing key informant interviews with administrators of the integrated care program, data support providers, and mental and physical health care providers, described in Table 1. Interview guides were created for each group of key informants. Interviews lasted approximately 30–90 minutes. Most individuals were interviewed only once with the exception of the Director of Missouri Department of Mental Health (MDMH) and the data management support consultant. The interview team consisted of a lead interviewer and a note taker. Interview notes were transcribed into a common database and reviewed by the research team. The team met regularly to review the interview notes and identify common themes. In addition, we conducted a document review of historical documents provided by the MDMH and their data support consulting organization regarding the progression of their program over time. A draft timeline and diagram of the MDMH integrated care approach was then presented to the MDMH

Table 1. Key Informant Interviews.

Area of Focus	Job	No. of Interviewees
Mental health	Administrative	2
	Provider	2
Primary care	Administrative	1
	Provider	2
Data	Coordinator	1

Director who reviewed these documents with the research team to answer any remaining questions and confirm details.

Structure of the Integrated Care in Missouri

CMHCs in Missouri currently function as health homes and are responsible for providing mental health care and coordinating physical health care for individuals with SMI. Health homes were also created with a primary care focus but provide a different type of integrated care and so are not the focus of this article. A more detailed description of the entire Missouri program, including its history and evolution, is available elsewhere (Wickizer, Sieck, & Geist, 2014). Fig. 1 provides an overview of the program's structure. Overall administration of the integrated care program in Missouri is provided by a committee of the MDMH, the Missouri Department of Medicaid (MoNet), the Missouri Primary Care Association (for physical health care providers), and the Missouri Coalition of Community Mental Health Centers (for mental health care providers). This committee is under the direction of the Medical Director for the MDMH. Most CMHCs utilize a collaborative care model in which the health home coordinates care with a physical health care provider to provide for the physical health care needs of individuals with SMI. Staffing levels are in accordance with the CMS definition of health homes and includes a director, nurse care manager, primary care consulting physician, community support specialist, and clerical services. CMHCs as health homes receive a greater CMS match than non-health homes as long as they can certify that they are providing appropriate health home services.

Population Health Management Elements in the Missouri Model

As the integrated care program in Missouri evolved, specific elements of PHM served to provide structure and facilitate adoption of new physical health tasks by CMHCs. An important first step was to define a target population. Working with a consulting data management company, MDMH developed criteria by which Medicaid enrollees would be automatically enrolled in a CMHC as their health home. This included all enrollees with: (1) a SMI diagnosis, (2) mental health condition plus substance use disorder, or (3) mental health condition and/or substance use plus one other chronic condition. Following identification of eligible enrollees,

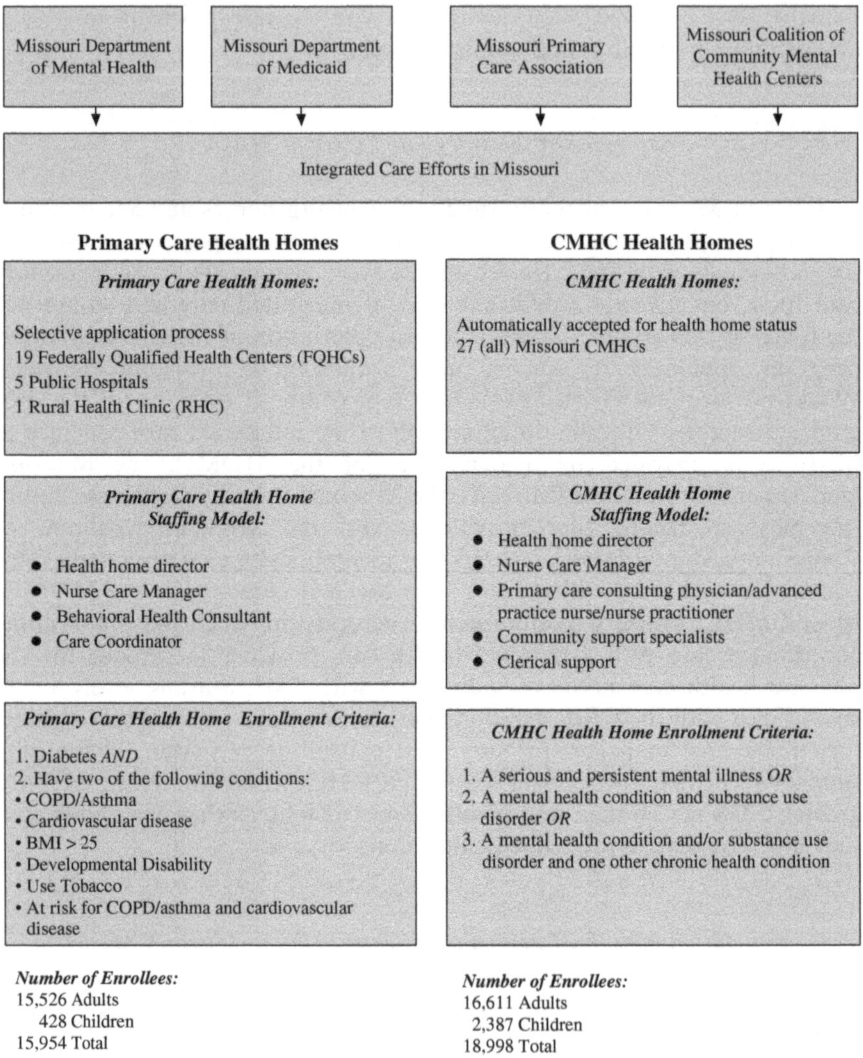

Fig. 1. Structure of MDMH Mental and Physical Health Homes.
Source: MDMH, 2013

MDMH assigned each enrollee to the CMHC from which they had previously sought the most care. For those enrollees who had not accessed services in any one particular location, MDMH proactively assigned these individuals to the health home nearest to their home address. This was an innovative step, nicknamed the DM3700 because of the original number of individuals identified. Each CMHC was responsible for reaching out to their assigned individuals and engaging them in the same way they would with established patients. The process required some adjustments as CMHCs attempted to contact individuals. Some were no longer eligible for Medicaid and therefore not in the health home program or who moved and were assigned to another CMHC.

This list was then provided to the CMHCs as their defined population for which they were responsible. Assigning responsibility was a critical new step. Previously, CMHCs would provide care for those who sought out their services. Under the PHM approach, CMHCs were required to engage all enrollees on their list and make sure they received a physical health screening to identify their risks of diabetes, obesity, and metabolic syndrome. While including a focus on physical health was new for mental health care providers, reaching out to individuals in this manner, and in some cases visiting their homes, was not a new concept. Rather, it was another application of working with patients who need more intensive assistance. This helped the program to gain acceptance among CMHCs.

Once the target population was identified, MDMH moved on to the next step of PHM: implementing and managing the process. Administration and direction was provided directly from leadership within MDMH, MoNet, and directors of the Primary Care and CMHC associations. Their approach was to direct funding toward specific initiatives that would encourage the provision of integrated care before the health home program was established, as well as during its implementation. In addition, they created a statewide database to which CMHCs would report required measures and which would track Medicaid claims. The MDMH Medical Director used this database to monitor progress of each CMHC as well as for the program as a whole and provided feedback throughout the process. However, the program administration did not mandate how integrated care was provided by the CMHCs. They provided resources, training, and on-going feedback but allowed the individual CMHCs to tailor their own programs to their population's needs. As one CMHC director stated, "*We are responsible for ensuring our patients are receiving the care they need ... taking that ownership when patients are not interested or feel that this does not impact their lives.*"

A third key element of PHM that is part of the MO IC program involved integrating critical factors including physical health measures, incentives, and use of information technology. First, because providing integrated care within a mental health care system involves the collection of data not previously tracked by CMHCs, the integrated care program established a set of physical health measures to be included in a metabolic screening that were reported and monitored throughout the program. These measures included having completed the metabolic screening, height, weight, blood pressure, lipid profile, HgA1C, smoking status, and psychiatric meds follow up with a primary care provider. These measures were used to assess the health risks of the population and to monitor progress toward health risk screening and health improvement goals. MDMH established measures of success and provided evaluation at 12 and 18 months into the program. These included medication adherence, biometric measures, as well as more subjective assessment from practice coaches.

A second important PHM component of establishing an integrated care program was use of health information technology. In 2011, MDMH contracted with an outside data support consulting agency to create the data infrastructure necessary to support the integrated care program implemented in the CMHCs (primary care health homes reported data to a separate organization). This organization was charged with developing a database that drew upon Medicaid claims data and elements reported by the CMHCs related to physical health. Both CMHCs and MDMH administration used this data set to compile regular reports to track their progress in screening and follow up for physical health issues at the CMHC level as well as program wide. At the time the program was established, use of electronic health records in the CMHCs was not widespread. Therefore, the creation of this database was a critical step to allow tracking of progress toward specific goals and to identify CMHC-level population needs. One director described the concept of providing integrated care prior to and after implementation of the data support system as "*Holistic as theory but now we are thinking about what that really means.*"

Finally, program administration utilized various incentives for addressing physical health issues leading up to and during full implementation. In a typical PHM structure, incentives are used to motivate program participants to take health improvement measures. In this case, incentives served to motivate CMHCs to provide integrated care to their patients. For example, as an early step, MDMH provided funds set aside for CMHCs to partner with Federally Qualified Health Centers (FQHCs). Under this arrangement, CMHCs could purchase services from FQHCs for physical health care services and FQHCs could purchase mental health care services from CMHCs. This allowed both organizations to develop reciprocal relationships that would become even more important as the integrated care program in Missouri progressed. Another incentive came once the program was established. CMHCs were established as health homes and therefore able to receive a higher Federal Medicaid match for health home services provided to their patients.

MDMH created the data infrastructure, selected the physical health measures to be included, and provided the motivation via program incentives set up as a structure through which CMHCs could begin to systematically address the physical health care needs of their patients with SMI. However, MDMH left the choice of how to address those needs up to the individual CMHC. Some CMHCs utilized the physical health data reports provided by the data management consulting agency to design interventions with their population. For example, upon learning that diabetes was the most prevalent risk factor, a CMHC may decide to provide additional training to staff to help them improve their follow up with these patients, and to patients to address this risk. Some CMHCs took the approach of devoting one month to each physical health issue, cycling through issues throughout the year. As one CMHC director said, "*Having a formal system has allowed for that process [Integrated Care] to start taking form, more of a structured format with specific things we are trying to accomplish, which keeps us on our path.*" Another director commented on not only the availability of data but the flexibility to use it to best meet the needs of their own population: "*From a programming standpoint, we can decide what services to offer, who to collaborate with, to work on certain metrics.*"

DISCUSSION

PHM provided a useful framework for Missouri to implement an integrated mental and physical health care program. Significant elements included defining a target population, selecting and monitoring appropriate measures, and determining intervention strategies CMHCs could employ in helping individuals with SMI manage their physical health concerns. The interviewees we spoke with expressed support for this program. They recognized the challenges involved but also appreciated the opportunity to address the health care needs of their population more comprehensively than had been previously possible.

Framing this program through the lens of PHM helped CMHCs to adjust because they could understand the approach. One interviewee summed this up as, "*those with the highest risk get the most attention.*" Interviewees from CMHCs stated that prior to the availability of this system, they were aware of their clients' physical health concerns but in a more anecdotal fashion. Directors commented that "*agencies get a lot more data. We use it to identify people who are lagging behind or to identify data issues.*" With this statewide data system, they were able to document physical health concerns and establish a regular means for addressing these issues. For example, one CMHC director discussed a recurring monthly focus on a particular disease. Each month, they would create a report identifying all individuals with that physical health concern, assess their status for necessary screening and follow up, and contact those individuals who needed to address that particular issue.

As noted earlier, the integrated care project leadership also provided resources to support their initiatives. They offered targeted funding for various projects as well as resources such as data and analytic support. This allowed providers, both on the physical and mental health side, to understand the priorities of the IC program and also to feel empowered to implement the necessary changes within their own organization.

Finally, MDMH took an incremental approach, as stated by one agency director, "*You don't start out as a Health Home.*" Beginning with smaller scale programs, they allowed members of the various organizations to work together and learn each organization's roles and expertise but scoped within a manageable project. Over time, the organizations and individuals involved developed an understanding of both the data relevant to their organization and of the power of working collaboratively. This incremental strategy also helped to facilitate an environment of trust as the project moved forward and built up to projects that were larger in scope. A physical health care provider stated it this way, "*It was the experience with those [initiatives] that framed what we were doing with this initiative.*"

CONCLUSION

The integrated care program currently underway in Missouri offers some guidance for the health home program as it becomes established nationwide. Many other states are at various stages of implementing such a program, due in part to the additional funds made available to health homes. CMS structure has already established staffing models. Models for establishment of a statewide data system exist and are available for purchase. Additional funding for providing integrated care is available for CMHCs that can be certified as health homes. CMHCs support this effort and are independently working toward it, demonstrating momentum in this movement. Examining the details of the Missouri program, particularly within a population health management framework, may provide additional guidance on how to harness and focus that momentum.

ACKNOWLEDGMENTS

The authors wish to acknowledge funding from the Ohio Department of Mental Health.

REFERENCES

Collins, E., Tranter, S., & Irvine, F. (2012). The physical health of the seriously mentally ill: An overview of the literature. *Journal of Psychiatric and Mental Health Nursing*, *19*(7), 638–646.

Colton, C. W., & Manderscheid, R. W. (2006). Congruencies in increased mortality rates, years of potential life lost, and causes of death among public mental health clients in eight states. *Preventing Chronic Disease*, *3*(2), 1–14.

Croft, B., & Parish, S. L. (2013). Care integration in the patient protection and affordable care act: Implications for behavioral health. *Administration and Policy in Mental Health and Mental Health Services Research*, *40*(4), 258–263.

Druss, B. G., Zhao, L., Von Esenwein, S., Morrato, E. H., & Marcus, S. C. (2011). Understanding excess mortality in persons with mental illness: 17-year follow up of a nationally representative US survey. *Medical Care*, *49*(6), 599.

Farnam, C. R., Zipple, A. M., Tyrrell, W., & Chittinanda, P. (1999). Health status risk factors: Of people with severe and persistent mental illness. *Journal of Psychosocial Nursing and Mental Health Services*, *37*(6), 16–21.

Garfield, R. L., Zuvekas, S. H., Lave, J. R., & Donohue, J. M. (2011). The impact of national health care reform on adults with severe mental disorders. *American Journal of Psychiatry*, *168*(5), 486–494.

Horvitz-Lennon, M., Kilbourne, A. M., & Pincus, H. A. (2006). From silos to bridges: Meeting the general health care needs of adults with severe mental illnesses. *Health Affairs (Millwood)*, *25*(3), 659–669.

Institute for Health Technology Transformation. (2012). *Population health management: A roadmap for provider-based automation in a new era of healthcare*. New York, NY: Institute for Health Technology Transformation.

Kilbourne, A. M., Morden, N. E., Austin, K., Ilgen, M., McCarthy, J. F., Dalack, G., & Blow, F. C. (2009). Excess heart-disease-related mortality in a national study of patients with mental disorders: Identifying modifiable risk factors. *General Hospital Psychiatry*, *31*(6), 555–563.

McAlearney, A. S. (2002). Population health management in theory and practice. *Advances in Health Care Management*, *3*, 117–159.

Mechanic, D. (2012). Seizing opportunities under the affordable care act for transforming the mental and behavioral health system. *Health Affairs (Millwood)*, *31*(2), 376–382.

Medicaid.gov. (2014). *Health homes* [Internet]. Retrieved from http://www.medicaid.gov/Medicaid-CHIP-Program-Information/By-Topics/Long-Term-Services-and-Support/Integrating-Care/Health-Homes/Health-Homes.html

Parks, J., Svendsen, D., Singer, P., Foti, M. E., & Mauer, B. (2006). *Morbidity and mortality in people with serious mental illness*. National Association of State Mental Health Program Directors (NASMHPD), Medical Directors Council Alexandria, VA.

Roshanaei-Moghaddam, B., & Katon, W. (2009). Premature mortality from general medical illnesses among persons with bipolar disorder: A review. *Psychiatric Services*, *60*(2), 147–156.

Wickizer, T., Dembe, A., Tanenbaum, S., Phelps, L., Sieck, C., & Geist, L. (2011). *Feasibility study and needs assessment: Integrating health care for high mortality general medical conditions with every day treatment*. Final report submitted to the Ohio Department of Mental Health, Center for HOPES.

Wickizer, T., Sieck, C. J., & Geist, L. (2014). *Best practices for providing integrated mental and physical healthcare: A review and case study*. Columbus, OH: Ohio Department of Mental Health.

POPULATION, COMMUNITY, AND PUBLIC HEALTH: MEASURING THE BENEFITS

Jason S. Turner and Connie Evashwick

ABSTRACT

Purpose – *Population, community, and public health notions are addressed separately in the Patient Protection and Affordable Care Act (ACA), have different foci and stakeholders, build on different frameworks to achieve their aims, and apply different measures to determine the long-term impact of interventions. This paper attempts to clarify each concept and proposes a method of evaluating each of these sets of health-related activities based on the benefits that accrue to the respective stakeholders.*

Approach – *In addition to indicating how to affect change and improvements in health, the ecological model of health also provides insight into how the benefits from health-related activities may or may not flow back to the entities sponsoring health interventions. By clearly defining each of the concepts and examining the methods and metrics being used to select activities and measure benefits, a valuation model is developed that measures the financial impact on the targeted population as well as the sponsoring institution.*

Population Health Management in Health Care Organizations
Advances in Health Care Management, Volume 16, 151–169

ISSN: 1474-8231/doi:10.1108/S1474-823120140000016007

Findings – *Defining, measuring, and evaluating are important to bring clarity to how individual organizations can contribute to the overall health of the population, as well as the limits of any single organization in doing so. Collective and upstream action will be required to improve the population's health, but identifying and justifying the role of each participating organization is a challenge that still lacks an overarching vision that can be explained and measured to the satisfaction of all stakeholders.*

Value – *Decision makers must justify how resources are committed in an era of scarcity and limited financial means. Moreover, methods must be in place to measure the impact of potential collaborations. The proposed valuation framework lays out the natural incentives, the responses to those incentives, and how to select initiatives that maximize value from the perspective of the various stakeholders.*

Keywords: Population health; community health; public health; measurement of benefits; return on investment (ROI)

The upheavals in the health care system have brought attention to three swirls of activities: population health, community health, and public health. The Patient Protection and Affordable Care Act (ACA), Internal Revenue Service (IRS), Public Health Accreditation Board (PHAB), and Institute of Medicine (IoM), among other government and private forces, are calling for or mandating an expansion of traditional roles, "upstream" interventions to prevent rather than cure disease, and collaboration with new partners. As health care entities attempt to respond, boards of trustees and directors are asking health care executives for justifications of resource allocation and measures of benefits and return on investment (ROI) of these new types of activities.

Efforts in population health, community health, and public health are all being pursued – but these concepts are in a state of conflation. Each of these notions is distinct. Each is addressed separately in the ACA, carries with it different foci and stakeholders, builds on different frameworks to achieve its aims, and applies different measures to determine the long-term impact of an intervention. The current confusion of what each concept means presents challenges to those leading changes who must justify their decisions by explaining what benefits accrue to whom. This paper intends to (1) clearly define population, community, and public health; (2) examine the methods and metrics being used to select activities and measure benefits; and (3) suggest approaches to determining valuation that enables decision makers to determine how to commit resources, assess the potential of collaborative efforts, and evaluate the relative benefit of new initiatives.

DEFINITIONS

Population Health is a misnomer, as the term has been used to refer not to the entire population, but to clearly defined sub-sets. Population health has been defined as "the health outcomes of a group of individuals, including the distribution of such outcomes within the group" (Kindig, 2007; Kindig & Stoddart, 2003). In 2013, the Institute of Medicine conducted a Roundtable, and has since been conducting regional meetings, to explore the concept and its application. Given unresolvable discrepancies, the IoM has adopted the Kindig and Stoddart definition (Institute of Medicine [IoM], 2013). Population health models and measurements are well established (McAlearney, 2003), but until recently have been highly focused and used more by insurers than providers. Jacobson and Teutsch (2012) have suggested the terminology of "total population health" to refer to all individuals in a given target area, thereby reinforcing that the above-mentioned definition of population health is indeed limited in its focus.

As a result of the ACA, population health management has become the strategic mantra of many health systems. Hospital readmission penalties, implementation of Medicare shared risk arrangements, accountable care organizations, and the movement towards more coordinated care models have necessarily pushed the notion of population health management to the forefront of health system innovations (CMS, 2014b). Reimbursement models are now rewarding (or at least not penalizing) hospitals and health systems for keeping their respective populations healthy, coordinating care, and using less costly health care delivery mechanisms (CMS, 2014a). Hospitalizations and utilization that are avoided translate directly to improved margins for hospitals and physicians. To realize both improved financial viability and health outcomes, entities are employing population health tools such as disease, lifestyle, disability, and integrated care management to improve health status and increase efficient use of appropriate resources. The individual members of the target population can be identified, an evaluation of an intervention typically has both a known numerator and a denominator, and the results are often viewed as the impact on utilization or costs.

Community Health the recent focus on the concept of community health is at least in part an outgrowth of the increased attention the IRS has paid to not-for-profit hospitals and health systems. Over the past 40 plus years, "community health" has been used in the United States to refer to a variety of programs, such as the "community health center" movement in the early 1970s, the "Healthy Communities" initiative sponsored by the Centers for Disease Control and Prevention (CDC), and the "community catalyst" recognition sponsored by the American Hospital Association. "Community" was either defined with regard to a specific program or left to each community to self-define. The recent focus derives from the federal interest in "community benefit" and the resulting mandate for hospitals to contribute to the community they serve.

"Community benefit" is the ruling in the federal tax code, mirrored by many states and local governments, which grants tax exemption to non-profit hospitals in exchange for benefits that they provide to the community. Although the initial IRS letter explaining tax exemption was written in 1964 and later codified in revenue rulings (Internal Revenue Service [IRS], 1969), not until 2009 (2008 was an optional reporting year) did the IRS mandate documentation for each non-profit hospital. Prior to ACA implementation, IRS efforts to quantify community benefit were exclusively focused on the costs to the hospital of providing the services – not on quantifying the benefits realized. The ACA attempted to tie community benefit to community health by requiring hospitals to perform community health needs assessments (CHNA), to develop community health improvement plans (CHIP), and, presumably in the future, to monitor relevant metrics to show the impacts community benefit activities have on community health (IRS, 2014). However, what constitutes the hospital's "community" remains to the hospital to define.

The IRS retains the responsibility for monitoring compliance with community benefit requirements. Although neither benchmarks nor enforcement criteria have yet been determined, a very specific list of reporting requirements is delineated in the annual report to the IRS, Form 990, Schedule H. In addition, 501(r) was also added to address the CHNA. The vast majority of community benefit dollars (85–90%) are spent by hospitals on charity care for patients with no or too little insurance. However, the IRS has categorized other ways that hospitals can contribute, including health promotion, education, community leadership development, and sundry other community-oriented efforts. Beyond the payment of direct services for individuals, the selected community might or might not be quantifiable (residents of a specific set of zip codes versus a target audience defined by cultural affinity or self-selection).

Public Health is the broadest of the three notions. The World Health Organization (WHO) and the Centers for Disease Control and Prevention (Centers for Disease Control and Prevention Foundation [CDCF], 2014) have defined public health as "those activities primarily geared toward the detection and control of infectious diseases, research for disease and injury prevention, and the promotion of healthy lifestyles." Since many public health programs are run by government, the target audience is most likely to be defined by the geographic area assigned to the government entity: a city, county, or even country. To achieve these aforementioned aims, public health professionals have concentrated on the 10 essential functions of public health (CDC, 2014).[1] Title IV of the ACA built upon these goals and functions by creating a national prevention, health promotion, and public health council to (1) coordinate federal activities across departments, (2) develop an "integrative health strategy that incorporates the most effective and achievable means of improving the health status of Americans and reducing the incidence of preventable illness and disability …", (3) provide recommendations concerning the most pressing health concerns, (4) "consider and propose evidence-based models, policies, and innovative approaches for the promotion of transformative models of prevention, integrative health, and public health on individual and community levels …, " and (5) establish a process for continual input from relevant stakeholders (PPACA, 2010).

In addition to the ACA, 2011 saw the launch of the PHAB (2014). For the first time in the history of the US public health activities, national accreditation guidelines were established in an effort to standardize and set a floor for the activities of state and local health departments. The standards include conducting (or participating in) a CHNA – just as non-profit hospitals are now required to do. Collaborations with organizations in the community, health education, disease prevention are also included – again, similar to categories identified by the IRS as appropriate for hospital community benefit activities.

Table 1 summarizes the differences in the three concepts as they relate to the US health care system at this point in time.

Table 1. Comparison of Population, Community, and Public Health.

	Mandates	Primary Entity	Target Audience	Quantification	Initiative Examples
Population health	ACA medicare, innovative models, payment	Hospital, health system, medical groups, health plans	Enrollees or members of a specific program	Numerator and denominator	Disease management programs for diabetes, asthma, etc.; employer wellness programs
Community health	IRS, ACA for CHNA and CHIP	Non-profit hospitals	Anyone affiliated by geography or personal characteristics with a prescribed community	Denominator could be vague; numerator might not be known	Health education programs, clinical and community health research or programs subsidized by the health care organization, carried out or supported for the express purpose of improving community health
Public health	ACA, PHAB	State and local public health departments; environmental health departments	All residents of an area targeted for a health initiative, often geographically defined	All residents of a specified area, often identified by census area related to a government agency	Monitoring of disease prevalence, food and water safety, or injury and violence prevention programs

STATEMENT OF THE PROBLEM

If the three concepts are so distinct, why is it that in practice, the lines appear to be blurred? In the current haste to respond to the ACA, health care organizations and other entities are enacting programs without necessarily considering the rationale, the evidence of long-term impact, or the measures that will be used to assess success. In order to achieve the goals of the Triple Aim, the plethora of activities generated in response to the ACA should be intentional, with measurable benefits for the organization initiating the activities in order to expect long-term sustainability. Moreover, collaboration among entities is essential to achieve a comprehensive approach that improves the overall health status of a population over an extended period of time (Kindig & Isham, 2014).

As an example, assume that hospitals, the public health department, the county Medicaid department for the state, and several community organizations collaborate on the CHNA required by both the IRS for non-profit hospitals and PHAB for the local health department to apply for accreditation. The result shows that 20% of the population has or is at risk for diabetes, which is thus one of the greatest health problems in the community.

To fulfill its community benefit requirements according to the ACA, one of the non-profit hospitals initiates an inpatient program to discharge patients with diabetes more quickly and link them with an outpatient-based diabetic follow-up clinic, with the goal of reduced length-of-stay and reduced readmissions. The public health department realizes that many diabetics are unaware of their condition, so it adds free monthly screenings at all of its outreach sites, with the goal of identifying more people with the condition. The Medicaid program seeks to save money by reducing the average cost/care for enrollees with diabetes, so it starts a weight loss program with a specific emphasis on healthy eating.

Fig. 1 shows how the concepts might overlap in a given community in implementing programs addressing the community need of diabetic care. None of the three initiatives address the "upstream factors" that lead to diabetes for the entire population of the county. Moreover, none of the organizations will be able to claim 100% success because of the "noise" brought about by the activities of the others. Nonetheless, all of the organizations are claiming to be working on the community's problem of high diabetes rates.

This type of conflation of intention is rampant across the country. One need only look at the many examples of conference presentations and webinars with "population health" or "community health" in the title to

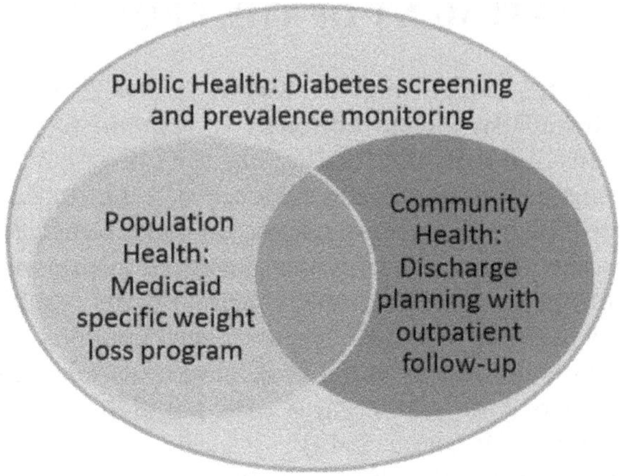

Fig. 1. Diabetic Interventions.

see that the extent of interest in these topics is matched only by the variation in measures being used to claim success.

ASSUMPTIONS

While the overlap between public, community, and population health activities might be significant, the method of determining the value associated with each of these concepts is distinct. The Institute for Healthcare Improvement has attempted to guide measurement of the concept of population health, along with the other two legs of the Triple Aim (Stiefel & Nolan, 2012). Their work includes suggested measures and sources of data, but they focus only on population health, not community or public health. Stoto (2013) acknowledges the overlap in the concepts in a white paper for Academy Health, but raises issues requiring research rather than suggesting solutions.

The Ecological Model of Health provides a framework for understanding how benefits (valuations) are viewed from different perspectives. The *Ecological Model of Health* is now widely understood and accepted by those in the health care delivery system as well as those in public health (McLeroy, Steckler, & Bibeau, 1988). After decades of increasingly sophisticated research, the myriad of factors that affect a person's health are understood to be more than medical care. Indeed, the health of an individual is attributed to genetics (10%), lifestyle (40%), family and social norms (20%), environment, including legal and regulatory parameters (20%), and only 10% to direct medical care (McGinnis, Williams-Russo, & Knickman, 2002).

The implications for measuring the success of a given program are obvious: no single entity in a community can take full credit for "preventing a disease," because too many relevant factors are beyond the control of any single organization. This means that health-related organizations serving any given target population must work together to impact the health status of that population, and no single entity can measure the impact of its activities without acknowledging the potential impact, positive or negative, of other entities affecting the same target population. Collaboration on needs assessment, interventions, and impact measurement become essential.

Upstream Prevention

Health care providers are also acknowledging more than ever before the need for "upstream prevention" – preventing deleterious health conditions from occurring rather than trying to cure patients once they have a condition. Individual health behavior warrants education and prevention one-on-one; a compatible community environment requires multi-institutional collaboration. Although the economic value of prevention has been recognized for centuries, only with the radical changes in payment methods instituted by the ACA have providers been given incentives to help patients prevent illness.

Particularly for health care providers, this change of paradigm also produces radical change in how "success" is measured. Whereas in the past, a hospital might measure success by the increase in number of admissions and patient days, under new pay-for-performance payment methods, the same hospital might now be rewarded as part of an Accountable Care Organization for decreased admissions and fewer days of stay.

Sources of Evidence

In today's world of "evidence-based decision-making," all health organizations are under scrutiny to justify their choice of activities. Although general agreement on this principle is widespread, the extent to which it is used varies. Moreover, the sources of evidence considered valid are different for clinical practice, public health, and community collaboration. The selection of evidence upon which to base an intervention is relevant to the outcomes that can be expected and measured. For example, physicians have now grown accustomed to adhering to the use of clinical guidelines, many of which have been generated through extensive consensus-building processes led or supported by the National Institutes of Health (NIH). Those working with community programs might use the Community Guide, a compendium of research studies that report on the usefulness of various preventive interventions (www.communityguide.org). Those focused on quality might draw from the assessments gathered by the Agency for Healthcare Research and Quality (AHRQ), while those working in public health agencies might turn to the WHO for guidance. Even when there is consensus on a problem, if different sources are used to assess the benefits of potential interventions, the choices and outcomes measures can be different.

The Triple Aim, a concept originally presented by the Institute for Healthcare Improvement, emphasizes improving the health care delivery system by reducing costs, enhancing the patient's experience, and advancing the health status of the entire population (IHI, 2014). These ideas were incorporated into the ACA. However, the terms were not well defined and became obscured once buried within the 2000+ pages of the ACA legislation (Kindig & Isham, 2014).

MEASURING VALUE

As noted above, the method of determining the value associated with each of these concepts of population, community, and public health is distinct.

Population Health Valuation

For hospitals and health systems interested in improving population health, the health administrators must pay attention to whom the benefits of improved health care outcome inure. For example, a hospital that invests in a population health management intervention will only realize a portion of the benefits. The target population will benefit from improved health but the hospital will incur the full costs of the intervention. Those costs are offset by improved population health only if the population health improvements translate to higher contribution margins on shared risk arrangements or a reduction in the potential readmission penalty. The analysis is complicated by having to calculate the marginal impact the intervention would have on existing lines of business outside of shared risk arrangements. The intervention may drive down readmissions but it may concomitantly drive down first time admissions that carry positive contribution margins. From the hospital perspective, the present value (PV) costs of a population health management intervention, to account for time value of money, and the PV of marginal effects to existing lines of business must be offset by the PV of direct benefits that inure to the hospital or health system (Eq. 1).[2] There may huge benefits for the population but if those benefits do not offset direct and marginal costs, then administrators may decide not to continue the population health management intervention.

$$\begin{aligned}&\text{Value of population health initiative}\\&\quad = \text{PV of hospital benefits} - \text{PV of intervention costs}\\&\quad - \text{PV of marginal, incidental costs to}\\&\qquad \text{existing lines of business}\end{aligned} \tag{1}$$

Community Health

The valuation of community benefit to a non-profit hospital is completely separate from the benefits that accrue to the communities served by the hospital. The IRS, which oversees CB reporting and the completion of community health improvement activities, values the cost of the intervention rather than the benefit that it generates (IRS, 2010). The rationale is that government extends tax exemption to hospitals and health systems in exchange for services rendered to the community for which the government would otherwise be responsible (*Bob Jones Univ. v. United States*, 1983; Gustafsson, 1996). There is no requirement to maximize the social or health-related wellbeing of the community. The community benefit activities only have to address needs identified in the CHNA regardless of social impact. IRS valuation of community benefit activities is clearly articulated in the Schedule H instructions associated with the Form 990 required of all not-for-profit hospitals and health systems.

$$\begin{aligned}&\text{Value of community benefit}^3 = \text{Cost of proving CB}\\&\quad - \text{Associated revenue that may be generated}\\&\quad\ \text{as a result of CB activities}\end{aligned} \tag{2}$$

The financial value to the non-profit hospital is the potential risk of losing its tax exemption, should the IRS decide to enforce a specific dollar amount of community benefit contributions. However, the valuation of the impact CB activities have on communities much more closely resembles the valuation of public health interventions to be discussed later. To value community health improvements, dollars are associated with the improved health outcomes, reduced disease prevalence, or other social benefits using one of three approaches (Wheeler & Clement, 1990) given below; however, the calculations assume that the number of people who comprise "the community" can be counted:

1. willingness to pay,
2. human capital, or
3. quality adjusted life year (QALY).

The willingness to pay approach determines the market's prevailing rate for the services being provided for free by a hospital. That rate is then multiplied by the total number of times the service is rendered to the community. For example, a hospital-based community outreach program that delivers 1,000 free or heavily discounted flu shots would multiply the prevailing rate (\$31.99/dose) by 1,000 to estimate the value of the service to the community. The \$31,990 (\$31.99 × 1,000) value is relatively straightforward to calculate when the quantity of services and price of services can be easily determined.

$$\begin{aligned}&\text{Value of social benefit (willingness to pay)}\\&\quad=(\text{PV of market rate for service provided}\times\text{quantity of services})\\&\quad-\text{PV of associated revenue to providers that may be generated}\\&\qquad\text{as a result of activities}\end{aligned}\tag{3}$$

The human capital approach is desirable when determination of a prevailing market rate is not possible. Health education and outreach programs often fall under this approach. This particular method attempts to tie increased productivity or reduced absenteeism to the intervention. A dollar amount is then associated with the reduced absenteeism. For example, a hospital that provides health-oriented outreach programs to community organizations anticipates increasing workplace productivity by 5% because the workforce will miss fewer days. If 1,000 working individuals making an average of \$160/day attended the program, then the program improved the community health by \$8,000 (1,000 individuals × \$160/day × 5% improvement).

$$
\begin{aligned}
&\text{Value of social benefit (human capital)}\\
&\quad = (\text{Quantity of productive hours gained as a result of the intervention}\\
&\quad \times \text{PV of the dollar rate associated with the productive hour})\\
&\quad - \text{PV of associated revenue to providers that may be generated}\\
&\qquad \text{as a result of activities} \qquad (4)
\end{aligned}
$$

The quality adjusted life year approach is the least exact and is the most difficult to accurately project. Under this approach an intervention is tied to the extension of life for an individual or a population receiving the intervention. It requires estimating the quality of the extended life (adjusted to reflect ability to perform the activities of daily life), the value of a year of life, and the timing of when that life extension occurs. Finally, because the benefits may not occur for many years, the value of that life extension is discounted to adjust for factors that impact the time value of money (inflation, opportunity costs, time preference for consumption, and risk). An example of this approach would be an outreach program that targets and reduces the prevalence of childhood diabetes in an identified pool of 150 twelve-year-old children. As a result of intervention, it is projected that the targeted population will live one extra year. Instead of living to an average of 75 years old, the 150 children are projected to live to an average of 76 years old. Although there is wide variance on health economists' financial value of one additional year, current estimates of one additional year of life are in the \$100,000 realm (Hirth, Chernew, Miller, Fendrick, & Weissert, 2000). Adjusting for 54 years of inflation at 2.5% would make the value of the life at the time it is realized somewhere around \$379,000. This additional \$379,000 is then multiplied by the 150 individuals receiving the intervention because the extra year of life is the average over the entire intervention population. The resulting \$56.85 million is a very large number that then needs to be discounted back in time at the typical required returns of equity rather than debt holders (Wheeler & Clement, 1990).[4] Assuming a 12% discount rate that is in line with historical equity returns in equity markets, the \$56.85 million has a current value of \$125,013. The reliance on assumptions and the predictions of when benefits are realized can greatly impact valuations. Although a valid method for valuing the social impact, the quality adjusted life year approach should be the valuation method of last resort as a result of the uncertainties associated with the required assumptions.

$$\begin{aligned}&\text{Value of social benefit (quality adjusted life year)}\\&\quad=(\text{Quantity of quality adjusted life years added as a result of the intervention}\\&\quad\times \text{PV of dollar rate associated with the year of life added})\\&\quad-\text{PV of associated revenue to providers that may be generated}\\&\quad\ \ \text{as a result of activities}\end{aligned} \tag{5}$$

Public health valuations are the most holistic approach. This valuation technique includes the health benefits that accrue to the community but it also accounts for the costs of providing the care. To accurately value public health initiatives, mapping the impact interventions have on the associated populations (using the three approaches already discussed) must be paired with the costs of providing the interventions. The costs of providing the public health intervention should be outweighed by the associated benefits. For example, the costs of a health education program (mentioned in the human capital approach to the valuation of social goods) must be less than $8,000 in benefits generated from the program. This framework allows public health professionals to begin differentiating between interventions based on the associated value (Wheeler & Clement, 1990). High benefit interventions may be associated with high cost and consequently result in little overall value. During periods of scarce resources, decisions should be made to maximize the societal impact while minimizing costs.

Public health initiatives, however, also take into account who is actually paying the bill and which populations are benefiting. In many developing countries, for example, techniques that are known to be cost-effective in improving health are not employed because of the shortage of financial, manpower, and other resources – regardless of the potential benefit to individuals or to the population overall.

$$\begin{aligned}&\text{Value of public health intervention}\\&\quad=\text{PV of social benefits (see Eqs. (3 – 5))} - \text{PV of intervention costs}\\&\quad-\text{PV of associated revenue to public health entities}\\&\quad\ \ \text{that may be generated as a result of activities}\end{aligned} \tag{6}$$

Financial Valuation

The increased attention by administrators and policy makers to ROI measures should be lauded and can be accommodated using the frameworks above. However, ROI has a precise meaning in the financial world, and using ROI measures exclusively warrants caution. The measure does not take into account the time value of money, cannot quantify the overall benefit, and does not address scale. To illustrate the limitations, imagine two mutually exclusive projects. The first project costs $100 to offer and generates $1,000 in social benefits or benefits to the hospital. The associated ROI for the first project is 900% ((1,000 – 100)/100). The second project generates $9,000 in social benefits or benefits to the hospital and costs $1,000 to offer. The ROI on the second project is 800% ((9,000 – 100)/1,000). Based on the ROI measure, administrators should pursue the first option; however, if value is defined as the difference between the PV of benefits and PV of costs of the intervention then the second project generates substantially more value. The value associated with the first project is $900 while the second project generates $8,000 in total value. The ROI measures can be an important decision tool but should be supplemented with net present value (NPV) or annualized NPV (ANPV) metrics moving forward. The NPV and ANPV tools will account for the timing of when the benefits are realized, will quantify the overall impact to the associated parties, can accommodate mutually exclusive projects with different durations, and will always identify the project with the largest value.

IMPLICATIONS

The conflation of terms described above leads to recommendations for practitioners, as well as for researchers and those charged with program evaluation. What organizations consider to be "success" depends upon their institutional goals. How programs are selected, evaluated and sustained or discontinued should relate to the institution's strategic plan, not be hasty reactions to external forces. Yet, we find that health care organizations, and hospitals in particular, are engaging in a wide variety of initiatives that are ostensibly related to the Triple Aim of improving population health, but in reality are designed to accomplish something quite different. How the value of these various activities is determined is problematic if the right logic models and measures are not applied from the outset.

If the goal is to improve total population health, then a clearer understanding of how population, community, and public health are defined and measured by their respective stakeholders is imperative. Pursued in isolation, the impact of any one component is limited. It is essential that entities leverage their particular strengths, respond to their natural incentives, and coordinate to optimize outcomes. However, coordination and leveraging can only occur when stakeholders are not being asked to perform activities that are outside of their natural incentive structure. Asking hospitals and health systems to pursue public health initiatives will only be fruitful when those initiatives work in concert with population or community health interventions that provide benefits back to the sponsoring entities.

The practical implications for health care executives translate into a structured set of questions to be asked of new population or community (benefit) activities:

Why are we initiating this project?
Who is the target audience?
What do we expect to accomplish?
Does the evidence base to date support the way in which we plan to conduct the activity and reinforce the expectations about results?
How will we measure success internally?
What other organizations in the community are working on this health problem?
Will our work complement, compete with, or undercut their work?
Could we partner with other organizations to have a better collective result?
Can we measure benefit to our organization as well as benefit to the aggregate?

If this simple list of essential questions is asked of each new initiative, measurable expectations and accountability will be more transparent. Those working in population health management for physician practices, hospitals, or managed care companies; those working on hospital community benefit programs; and those working on public health outreach programs will all have a clearer understanding of how their activities can fit together, for the overall improvement of the health of each population group and the business sustainability of each organization involved.

Similarly, understanding the differences among the three concepts and how to measure them has implications for researchers and those engaged in evaluation. Research methodologies, samples, variables, data sources, and databases of evidence must be based on the appropriate framework. Indeed, additional research and more detailed evaluation studies should contribute to clarifying the differences and overlaps of the three concepts of population, public, and community health.

Those engaged in making or evaluating policy should grasp that the ACA and other federal legislation and regulations have forced an artificial separation in the way health care organizations approach improving the health of the overall population. However, given that differences are now imbedded in laws and policies, awareness of the current conflation might help to improve future legislation.

CONCLUSIONS

This paper asserts that currently there are three swirls of programmatic interventions being directed at the health of individuals, aggregated by population, community, or the public. The concepts of population, community, and public health are different, but all have a role to play in improving the overall health of the United States. Administrators, clinicians, researchers, and policy makers must understand the distinctions among the concepts, particularly in light of the ACA. Defining, measuring, and evaluating are important to clarify how individual organizations can contribute to the overall health of the population, as well as the limits of any single organization in doing so. Collective and upstream action will be required to improve the population's health, but identifying and justifying the role of each participating organization is a challenge that still lacks an overarching vision that can be explained and measured to the satisfaction of all stakeholders. Clear definitions and acceptable measures are a good place to start.

NOTES

1. Monitoring of health status to identify community health problems, diagnosis and investigation of health problems and health hazards, mobilization of community partnerships to identify and solve health problems, development of policies and plans that support individual and community health efforts, enforcement of laws and regulations that protect health and ensure safety, linkage of people to needed personal health services and the provision of health care when otherwise unavailable, assurance of a competent public and personal health care workforce, evaluation of the effectiveness, accessibility, and quality of personal and population-based health services, research for new insights and innovative solutions to health problems, and the education and empowerment of people about health issues.
2. Because the financial benefits of population health accrue to hospitals, using the firm's cost of capital should be used to account for TVM.

3. There is no need to account for time value of money since the reporting of CB activities to the IRS typically takes place in the same year (or shortly thereafter) as the performance of the activity.

4. Using the required return to equity holders is appropriate since none of the benefits of extended life accrue to the institution's debt holders.

REFERENCES

Bob Jones Univ. v. United States, 461 U.S. 574, 588 1983.

Centers for Disease Control and Prevention (CDC). (2014). *The public health system and the 10 essential public health services*. Retrieved from http://www.cdc.gov/nphpsp/essentialservices.html

Centers for Disease Control and Prevention Foundation (CDCF). (2014). *What is public health?* Retrieved from http://www.cdcfoundation.org/content/what-public-health

Centers for Medicare & Medicaid Services (CMS). (2014a). *Shared savings program*. Retrieved from http://www.cms.gov/Medicare/Medicare-Fee-for-Service-Payment/sharedsavingsprogram/index.html?redirect=/

Centers for Medicare & Medicaid Services (CMS). (2014b). *Innovation center*. Retrieved from http://innovation.cms.gov/initiatives/#views=models

Gustafsson, L. (1996). The definition of "charitable" for federal income tax purposes: Defrocking the old and suggesting some new fundamental assumptions. *Houston Law Review*, *33*, 587–649.

Hirth, R. A., Chernew, M. E., Miller, E., Fendrick, A. M., & Weissert, W. G. (2000). Willingness to pay for a quality-adjusted life year: In search of a standard. *Medical Decision Making*, *20*(3), 332–342.

Institute for Healthcare Improvement (IHI). (2014). *Triple Aim*. Retrieved from http://www.ihi.org/Topics/TripleAim/Pages/default.aspx. Accessed on May 3, 2014.

Institute of Medicine. (2013). *Toward quality measures for population health and the leading health indicators*. Washington, DC: The National Academies Press.

Internal Revenue Service. (1969). *Revenue ruling* (pp. 68–545). Washington, DC: Internal Revenue Service.

Internal Revenue Service. (2010). Instructions for schedule H (Form 990). Washington, DC: Internal Revenue Service.

Internal Revenue Service (IRS). (2014). *New Requirements for 501(c)(3) Hospitals under the Affordable Care Act*. Retrieved from http://www.irs.gov/Charities-&-Non-Profits/Charitable-Organizations/New-Requirements-for-501(c)(3)-Hospitals-Under-the-Affordable-Care-Act

Jacobson, D., & Teutsch, S. (2012). *An environmental scan of integrated approaches for defining and measuring total population health by the clinical care systems, the government public health system, and stakeholder organizations*. Washington, DC: National Quality Forum. Retrieved from http://www.quality-forum.org/Publications/2012/06/An_Environmental_Scan_of_Integrated_Approaches_for_Defining_and_Measuring_Total_Population_Health.aspx,2012

Kindig, D. A., & Stoddart, G. (2003). What is population health? *American Journal of Public Health, 93*, 366–369.

Kindig, D. A. (2007). Understanding population health terminology. *Milbank Quarterly, 85*(1), 139–161.

Kindig, D. A., & Isham, G. (2014). Population health improvement: A community health business model that engages partners in all sectors. *Frontiers of Health Services Management, 30*(4), 3–20.

McAlearney, A. S. (2003). *Population health management: Strategies to improve outcomes.* Chicago, IL: Health Administration Press.

McGinnis, J. M., Williams-Russo, P., & Knickman, J. R. (2002). The case for more active policy attention to health promotion. *Health Affairs, 21*(2), 78–93.

McLeroy, K. R., Steckler, A., & Bibeau, D. (Eds.). (1988). The social ecology of health promotion interventions. *Health Education Quarterly*, 15(4), 351–377.

Public Health Accreditation Board. (2014). Retrieved from https://www.phab.org/

Stiefel, M., & Nolan, K. (2012). *A guide to measuring the Triple Aim: Population health, experience of care, and per capita cost.* IHI Innovation Series white paper. Cambridge, MA: Institute for Healthcare Improvement. Retrieved from www.IHI.org.

Stoto, M. (2013, February 21). Population health in the Affordable Care Act era. *Academy Health.* Retrieved from www.academyhealth.org/files/AH2013pophealth.pdf. Accessed on February 1, 2014.

The Patient Protection and Affordable Care Act (PPACA). (2010). Pub. L. No. 111-148, 124 *Stat*. 119. 2010. Mar 23.

Wheeler, J. R. C., & Clement, J. P. (1990). Capital expenditure decisions and the role of the not-for-profit hospital: An application of a social goods model. *Medical Care Review, 47*(4), 467–486.

SECTION IV
FACTORS IN PHM BEYOND THE MANAGEMENT OF HEALTH CARE ORGANIZATIONS

INVITED LETTER: THE EVOLVING MODEL OF HEALTH CARE IN THE UNITED STATES: SYSTEM CHANGE IS NOT ENOUGH

Randell K. Wexler

The cost of providing health care in the United States (US) is on a clearly unsustainable trajectory, and has been the subject of significant debate and transformational effort over the past few years. In 2013, health care expenditures were 17.3 percent of gross domestic product, consuming dollars that are no longer available for use elsewhere (Martin, Hartman, Whittle, & Catlin, 2014). In addition, despite expending $3 trillion annually on health care, the US ranks 27th in care of ischemic heart disease, 27th in care of hypertensive heart disease, 31st in diabetes care, and 32nd in chronic obstructive pulmonary disease management when compared to other Organization for Economic Cooperation and Development (OECD) countries (CMS; Murray et al., 2013).

The movement toward improving population health, defined as the health outcomes of a group of individuals, including the distribution of

Population Health Management in Health Care Organizations
Advances in Health Care Management, Volume 16, 173–176

ISSN: 1474-8231/doi:10.1108/S1474-823120140000016008

such outcomes within the group (Kindig & Stoddart, 2003), has seen the promulgation of health care delivery models such as Patient-Centered Medical Homes (PCMH) and Accountable Care Organizations (ACOs). Both have similar structural elements such as care coordination, proactive care (i.e., reaching out to the patient when care is due, not waiting for the patient to access the system), and the goal of managing populations of patients based on guideline recommendations and medical need. Although these models of care are necessary to improve population health (thereby reducing cost and improving outcomes) they are not in and of themselves sufficient to achieve the goals of ideal population health. The US health care system can change how insurance coverage is paid for, where the care is delivered, and how care is achieved, but without a fundamental change in how patients think about and access health care; the goal of reduced cost with improved outcomes will remain elusive.

To produce the desired results of affordable health care with improved outcomes, it is essential that patient behavior and social circumstance, currently ignored by policymakers and other stakeholders, be integrated into system change efforts. Unfortunately, the current policy assumption in primary care transformation is that a different health care delivery system can make patients proactively engage in their own care, make healthy choices, and learn to (and even desire to) manage their own health care needs and chronic conditions. This position ignores the individual needs, life experiences, and personal circumstances that are unique to each patient and usually contributes to a significant breakdown of the desired action at the level of the patient-physician dyad.

My colleagues and I have recently completed a study funded by the Agency for Healthcare Research and Quality (AHRQ) entitled: "Use of HIT to Increase Primary Care Access in Medicaid Patients." In this study, we embedded a patient scheduler in the emergency department (ED) of an Academic Health Center and arranged for patients with Medicaid coverage to schedule an appointment with a primary care physician of their choosing, at the time and date of their choice, and in the location most convenient for them. In essence, we sought to remove many system barriers to access, considered to be problematic for those insured by Medicaid. Despite this intervention, the vast majority of patients enrolled in this program did not establish a long-term relationship with a primary care physician, and continued to access the ED for non-urgent care. Subjects reported that their motives for their health service use patterns were strongly linked to socio-demographic issues. In the end, it is not just about the delivery system.

If those patients in greatest need cannot access it due to socio-demographic barriers, the availability of high-quality, low-cost health care is insufficient to address the problem.

At the same time, we need to raise patient awareness of how the health care delivery system works. As people who have never used insurance seek care under the new plans derived from efforts to improve coverage, there is a concomitant need to support improved health literacy – the degree to which individuals have the capacity to obtain, process, and understand basic health information and services needed to make appropriate health decisions (U.S. Department of Health and Human Services, 2000). What we experience now in EDs and primary care offices throughout the United States is misalignment between the patient's ability to negotiate complex health care systems and their expectations of both "how to" and "when to" use the system. This results in individuals seeking primary care in emergency settings, expectations for treatment and laboratory diagnostics that are preference or anecdotally-driven rather than evidence driven, and a host of other process issues that serve to promote bad medicine, costly care, and unrealistic patient demands.

For instance, there are growing concerns among practitioners that satisfaction is increasingly positioned as a definitive marker of quality. In fact, satisfied patients undergo more tests, have more hospital admissions, have higher costs, and experience higher mortality rates than less satisfied patients (Fenton, Jerant, Bertakis, & Franks, 2012). Tying a physician's reimbursement to non-evidence-based targets, such as a 30 day readmission rate less than the national average, ignores the evidence that these measures are not tied to quality of care, rather socio-demographic factors over which physicians and health systems have no control (Herrin et al., 2014). While efforts to improve quality of care are laudable, these markers have created a system where physicians adhere to patient preferences by overprescribing and focusing on the management of conditions for 30 days post admission as opposed to a focus on patients' long-term health care needs.

Reducing costs, improving experiences, and advancing population health are admirable goals. However, population health management requires that we not try and fix a broken system by adjusting only one part. Patient education, input, and stakeholder acknowledgment of non-health system factors that impact cost help patients to become responsible for managing their own care and are key factors in moving from the system we have now to the system we need.

ACKNOWLEDGMENT

This manuscript was funded in part by grant AHRQ (R21HS020693).

REFERENCES

CMS. National Health Expenditures. (2012). Highlights. Retrieved from http://www.cms.gov/Research-Statistics-Data-and-Systems/Statistics-Trends-and-Reports/NationalHealthExpendData/downloads/highlights.pdf. Accessed on August 26, 2014.

Fenton, J. J., Jerant, A. F., Bertakis, K. D., & Franks, P. (2012). The cost of satisfaction: A national study of patient satisfaction, health care utilization, expenditures, and mortality. *Archives of Internal Medicine. 172*(5), 405–411. doi:10.1001/archinternmed.2011.1662

Herrin, J., St. Andre, J., Kenward, K., Joshi, M. S., Audet, A. J., & Hines, S. C. (2014). Community factors and hospital readmission rates. The commonwealth fund. *Health Services Research*. Retrieved from http://www.commonwealthfund.org/Publications/In-the-Literature/2014/Apr/Community-Factors-and-Hospital-Readmission-Rates.aspx. Accessed on April 9, 2014.

Kindig, D., & Stoddart, G. (2003). What is population health? *American Journal of Public Health, 93*, 380–383. doi:10.2105/AJPH.93.3.380

Martin, A. B., Hartman, M., Whittle, L., & Catlin, A. (2014). National health spending in 2012: Rate of health spending growth remained low for the fourth consecutive year. *Health Affairs, 33*, 167–177. doi:10.1377/hlthaff.2013.1254

Murray, C. J. et al. (2013). For the US burden of disease collaborators. The state of US health, 1990–2010: Burden of diseases, injuries, and risk factors. *JAMA, 310*(6), 591–608.

U.S. Department of Health and Human Services. (2000). *Healthy people 2010: Understanding and improving health* (2nd ed.). Washington, DC: U.S. Government Printing Office.

PAYMENT MODELS TO SUPPORT POPULATION HEALTH MANAGEMENT

Timothy R. Huerta, Jennifer L. Hefner and Ann Scheck McAlearney

ABSTRACT

Purpose – *To survey the policy-driven financial controls currently being used to drive physician change in the care of populations*

Design/methodology/approach – *This paper offers a review of current health care payment models and discusses the impact of each on the potential success of PHM initiatives. We present the benefits of a multi-part model, combining visit-based fee-for-service reimbursement with a monthly "care coordination payment" and a performance-based payment system.*

Findings – *A multi-part model removes volume-based incentives and promotes efficiency. However, it is predicated on a pay-for-performance framework that requires standardized measurement. Application of this model is limited due to the current lack of standardized measurement of quality goals that are linked to payment incentives.*

Population Health Management in Health Care Organizations
Advances in Health Care Management, Volume 16, 177–183

ISSN: 1474-8231/doi:10.1108/S1474-823120140000016010

Practical implications – *Financial models dictated by health system payers are inextricably linked to the organization and management of health care.*

Originality/value – *There is a need for better measurements and realistic targets as part of a comprehensive system of measurement assessment that focuses on practice redesign, with the goal of standardizing measurement of the structure and process of redesign. Payment reform is a necessary component of an accurate measure of the associations between practice transformation and outcomes important to both patients and society.*

Keywords: Payment models; policy incentives; health care reform

While this volume of *Advances* speaks to how organizations are addressing the growing environmental demands to manage population health, there is a disconnect between the populations served and the aggregation of these populations to the level of public health. Population health management is not public health, but discourse in this issue suggests that these two words have become confounded. Further, there is an evolution of the belief that payment models alone can be used to shift the health of populations, and by extension, the public. There are a number of payment models under discussion as a part of payment reform, nationally, including capitation, shared savings, shared savings plus penalty, prospective payment, episodic payments, pay-for-performance, and hospital-physician bundling. Below we briefly describe each of these models, and follow with a discussion of a mixed model approach we propose to facilitate better population health management.

CAPITATION

Both of the shared savings programs have been optionally linked to additional care coordination payments. These payments have been made in support of preventive care to incentivize providers to engage in aggressive chronic disease management. This is in sharp contrast to capitation, where fee-for-service is replaced by flat payments plus bonuses and penalties. The provider organization assumes full risk for a defined patient population (Bobbit, 2011). The benefits of capitation are seen in AHRQ frontier organizations including Kaiser, Scott, and White (Texas) and Geisinger (Pennsylvania). These organizations created capture groups that funneled patient populations to insurance-company-owned hospital facilities. When these same ideas were brought to a non-integrated environment with insufficient data management capacity, the result created a backlash against capitation.

SHARED SAVINGS

Reimbursement is fee-for-service plus a portion of dollars saved relative to predicted costs, if quality and patient satisfaction are enhanced. In an "asymmetric" or "one-sided model," providers are incentivized to meet outcomes but not penalized for failing to meet them. Further, there have been concerns over the absence of risk adjustment in the target metrics, such that practices located in high socioeconomic status (SES) areas are privileged over their low SES analogs. The focus on population health incentivizes well-care and preventive services (Bobbit, 2011).

SHARED SAVINGS PLUS PENALTY

Concerned about the asymmetric model of shared savings, policy makers have explored including a sharing of increased costs concomitant with shared savings. In these approaches, policy makers have increased the value of the shared savings bonus to account for the increased risk. This approach is a "symmetric" or "two-sided model" (Bobbit, 2011).

PROSPECTIVE PAYMENT

In general use at hospitals, as defined by Centers for Medicare and Medicaid Services (CMS), prospective payment reimburses for inpatient hospital services based on a prepaid amount that covers a defined period of time. This approach uses the Diagnosis Related Group (DRG) system that bases payment on how the patient's disease is classified by CMS

(ASHA.org). While prospective payment is common in hospitals, it is not currently aligned with preventive care. In a patient-centered medical home (PCMH), prospective payment in chronic disease management differs from capitation in that each individual is risk scored and reimbursed according to the risk profile of the patient.

EPISODIC PAYMENTS

An alternative model that connects fee-for-service and bundling is reimbursement defined in terms of "episodes of care." Episodes of care may extend from time of admission to days or weeks after discharge. These episodes may include home health, extended care facility stays, or ancillary services (Mechanic, 2011). These models do not incentivize prevention or medical-home coordination, rather they focus on cost containment for either single or multiple care contacts related to both the episode and incidental engagements.

PAY-FOR-PERFORMANCE (P4P)

Pay-for-performance (P4P) ties an aspect of payment to the achievement of certain metrics that often include cost, but are not limited to it. In this way, P4P diverges from shared savings programs through the adoption of population-level outcome measures (e.g., number of patients immunized for a specific disease; attainment of desired clinical outcomes; achievement of high patient satisfaction scores) that advance a public health or cost containment goal (AHRQ.gov/P4P).

HOSPITAL-PHYSICIAN PAYMENT BUNDLING

The advent of Accountable Care Organizations has included the rise of hospital-physician bundling. Much like episodic care, reimbursement is based on the cost of a procedure or diagnosis. However, under this model, the bundled payment includes both the hospital and physician components of the cost. One payment is made for the collective services associated with an episode of care (Komisar, Feder, & Ginsburg, 2011).

A MODEL FOR BETTER POPULATION HEALTH MANAGEMENT

Each of these approaches has had mixed results. The success of capitation in captive systems led many states and municipalities to attempt to adopt that model. However, the requisite need for data, a robust IT backbone and risk models, and a cultural shift among patients have undermined those efforts. As a result, the United States must explore the options for financing care that align with the financial, patient, and population outcomes it champions, in a context appropriate manner.

The major primary care physician groups and the Patient-Centered Primary Care Collaborative (PCPCC) believe that the most effective way to re-align payment incentives to support the PCMH, would be to combine traditional fee-for-service office visits with a multi-part model.

The first component of this model is a monthly care coordination payment ("bundled care coordination fee") for the physician and non-physician work that falls outside of a face-to-face visit and the system infrastructure (e.g., heath information technologies) needed to achieve better outcomes. Bundling of services into a monthly fee removes volume-based incentives and promotes efficiency when enmeshed in a P4P framework.

The prospective nature of care coordination payment recognizes the up-front costs to maintain the required level of care. Care coordination payments should be risk adjusted to ensure that there are no inherent incentives to avoid the treatment of the more complex, costly patients. In addition, this payment component should reflect the level of the practice's service capability based on the NCQA PPC-PCMH recognition process.

While effective chronic disease management and care coordination represents one component of care, there are also emergent needs generated by both chronic and non-chronic conditions. The ambulatory (outpatient care) setting includes urgent care services. To that end, the second component of PCMH funding is a visit-based, fee-for-service mode. This component recognizes that visit-based services maintain an incentive for the physician to see the patient in an office-visit setting when appropriate.

It is insufficient to paint the stick orange and call it a carrot. While some providers will react to penalties, early adopters are more likely to be moved by incentives and positive reinforcement and dis-incentivized by the lack of a cohesive measurement model. The state has a vested interest in aligning its health care system to national goals and quality measures, and to develop new measures in areas where such guidance is rare.

ADVANCING MEASUREMENT FOR POPULATION HEALTH MANAGEMENT

There are many current frameworks for studying the context of evidence-based health care innovations (Bodenheimer, Ghorob, Willard-Grace, & Grumbach, 2014; Fox et al., 2013; Lee, Teich, & Spurr, 1996; Singer et al., 2011), drawing upon existing health care management and innovations theory, and extensive qualitative field work (Sinsky et al., 2013; Chaudoir, Dugan, & Barr, 2013; Damschroder et al., 2009; Tomoaia-Cotisel et al., 2013). Efforts to identify measures of context in the field of health innovations have entailed developing a framework based on theory and/or field work and then searching the literature for corresponding measures (Chaudoir, Dugan, & Barr, 2013) or developing a list of example elements (Tomoaia-Cotisel et al., 2013).

We must have a clear definition of success. The lack of consensus across existing studies suggests that the field is fragmented and that there is a need for the development of a comprehensive, practice-based approach to surveying the diversity of transformation innovations. As detailed in the above section, researchers have developed instruments to track and measure transformation to PCMH, and these instruments have been modified and adapted in various studies. However, these instruments were not developed using a rigorous measurement development methodology, and adaptation is occurring without standardization.

We need better measurements and realistic targets as part of a comprehensive system of measurement assessment that focuses on practice redesign, with the goal of standardizing measurement of the structure and process of redesign. This step is necessary for the field to begin to accurately measure the associations between practice transformation and outcomes important to both patients and society.

REFERENCES

Bobbit, J. J. (2011). *The family physicians ACO blueprint for success.* Smith Anderson LLC. Medicare prospective payment systems: A summary [Internet]. Retrieved from http://www.asha.org/practice/reimbursement/medicare/pps_sum.htm

Bodenheimer, T., Ghorob, A., Willard-Grace, R., & Grumbach, K. (2014). The 10 building blocks of high-performing primary care. *Annals of Family Medicine*, *12*(2), 166–171.

Chaudoir, S. R., Dugan, A. G., & Barr, C. H. I. (2013). Measuring factors affecting implementation of health innovations: A systematic review of structural, organizational, provider, patient, and innovation level measures. *Implementation Science*, *8*(1), 22.

Damschroder, L. J., Aron, D. C., Keith, R. E., Kirsh, S. R., Alexander, J. A., & Lowery, J. C. (2009). Fostering implementation of health services research findings into practice: A consolidated framework for advancing implementation science. *Implementation Science*, *4*, 50. doi:10.1186/1748-5908-4-50

Fox, C. H., Vest, B. M., Kahn, L. S., Dickinson, L. M., Fang, H., Pace, W., … Peterson, K. (2013). Improving evidence-based primary care for chronic kidney disease: Study protocol for a cluster randomized control trial for translating evidence into practice (TRANSLATE CKD). *Implementation Science*, *8*, 88. doi:10.1186/1748-5908-8-88

Komisar, H., Feder, J., & Ginsburg, P. (2011, July). *"Bundling" payment for episodes of hospital care. Issues and recommendations for the new pilot program in medicare.* Washington, DC: The Center for American Progress.

Lee, F., Teich, J. M., & Spurr, C. D. (1996). Bates DWCP. Implementation of physician order entry: User satisfaction and self-reported usage patterns. *Journal of the American Medical Informatics Association*, *3*, 42–55.

Mechanic, R. E. (2011). Opportunities and challenges for episode-based payment. *The New England Journal of Medicine*, *365*(9), 777–779.

Pay-for-performance (P4P): AHRQ resources [Internet]. Retrieved from http://www.ahrq.gov/qual/pay4per.htm

Singer, S. J., Burgers, J., Friedberg, M., Rosenthal, M. B., Leape, L., & Schneider, E. (2011). Defining and measuring integrated patient care: Promoting the next frontier in health care delivery. *Medical Care Research and Review*, *68*(1), 112–127.

Sinsky, C. A., Willard-Grace, R., Schutzbank, A. M., Sinsky, T. A., Margolius, D., & Bodenheimer, T. (2013). In search of joy in practice: A report of 23 high-functioning primary care practices. *Annals of Family Medicine*, *11*(3), 272–278. doi:10.1370/afm.1531

Tomoaia-Cotisel, A., Scammon, D. L., Waitzman, N. J., Cronholm, P. F., Halladay, J. R., Driscoll, D. L., Stange, K. C. (2013). Context matters: The experience of 14 research teams in systematically reporting contextual factors important for practice change. *Annals of Family Medicine*, *11*(Suppl. 1), S115–S123.